Jerusalem and Tel Aviv
Through the Looking Glass

A Photographic Exploration

Hae Won Shin

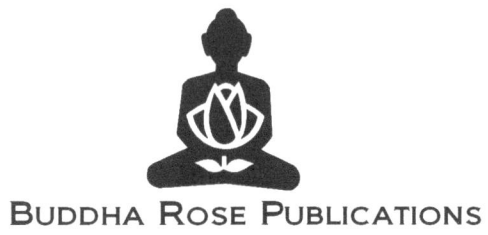

Buddha Rose Publications

Jerusalem and Tel Aviv Through the Looking Glass
Copyright © 2017 by Hae Won Shin
All Rights Reserved.

First Edition 2017

ISBN 10: 1-949251-02-0
ISBN 13: 978-1-949251-02-9

No part of this book may be reproduced in any manner without the expressed permission of the author or the publishing company.

Printed in the United States of America

10 9 8 7 6 5 4 3 2 1

Jerusalem

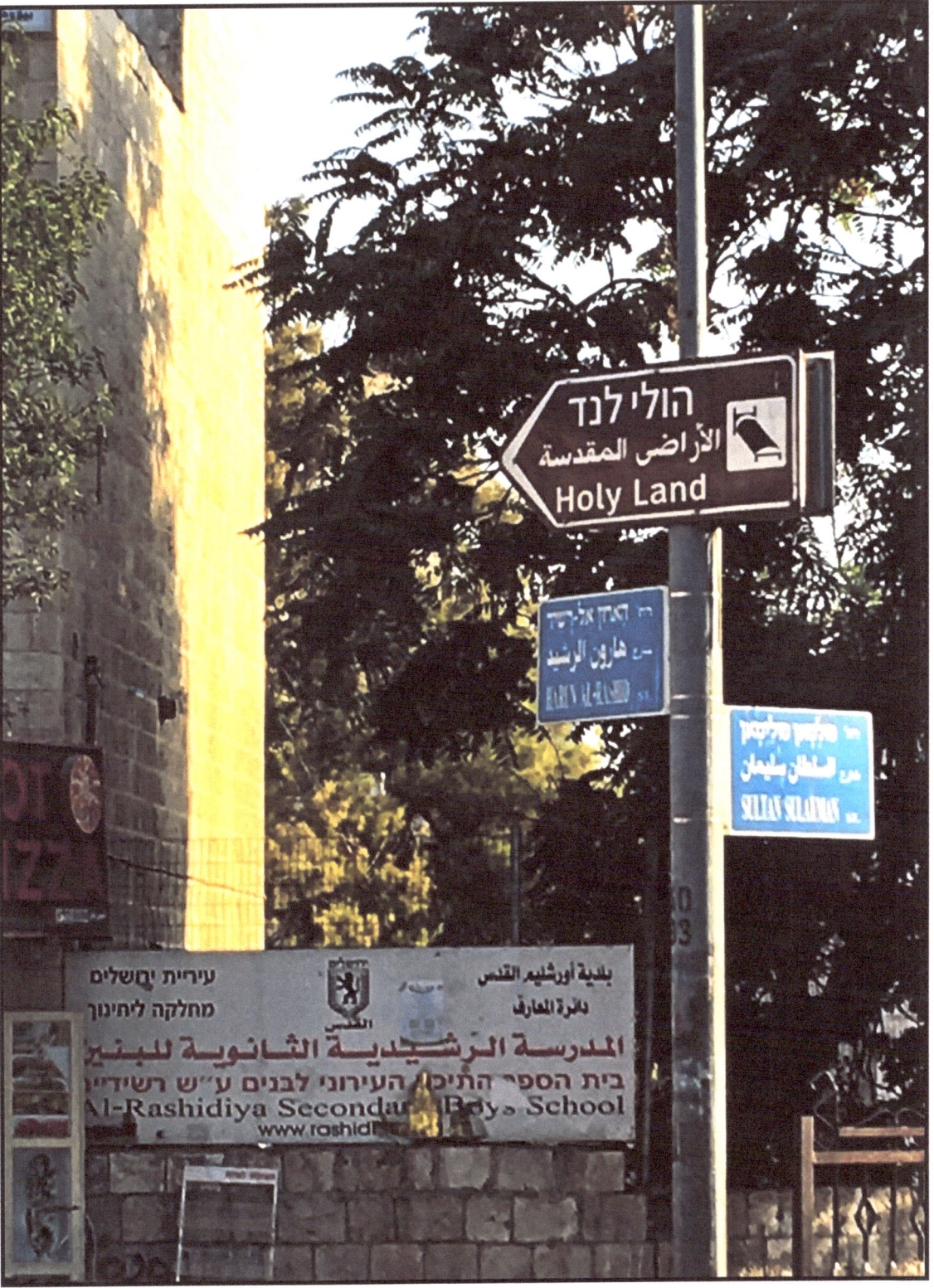

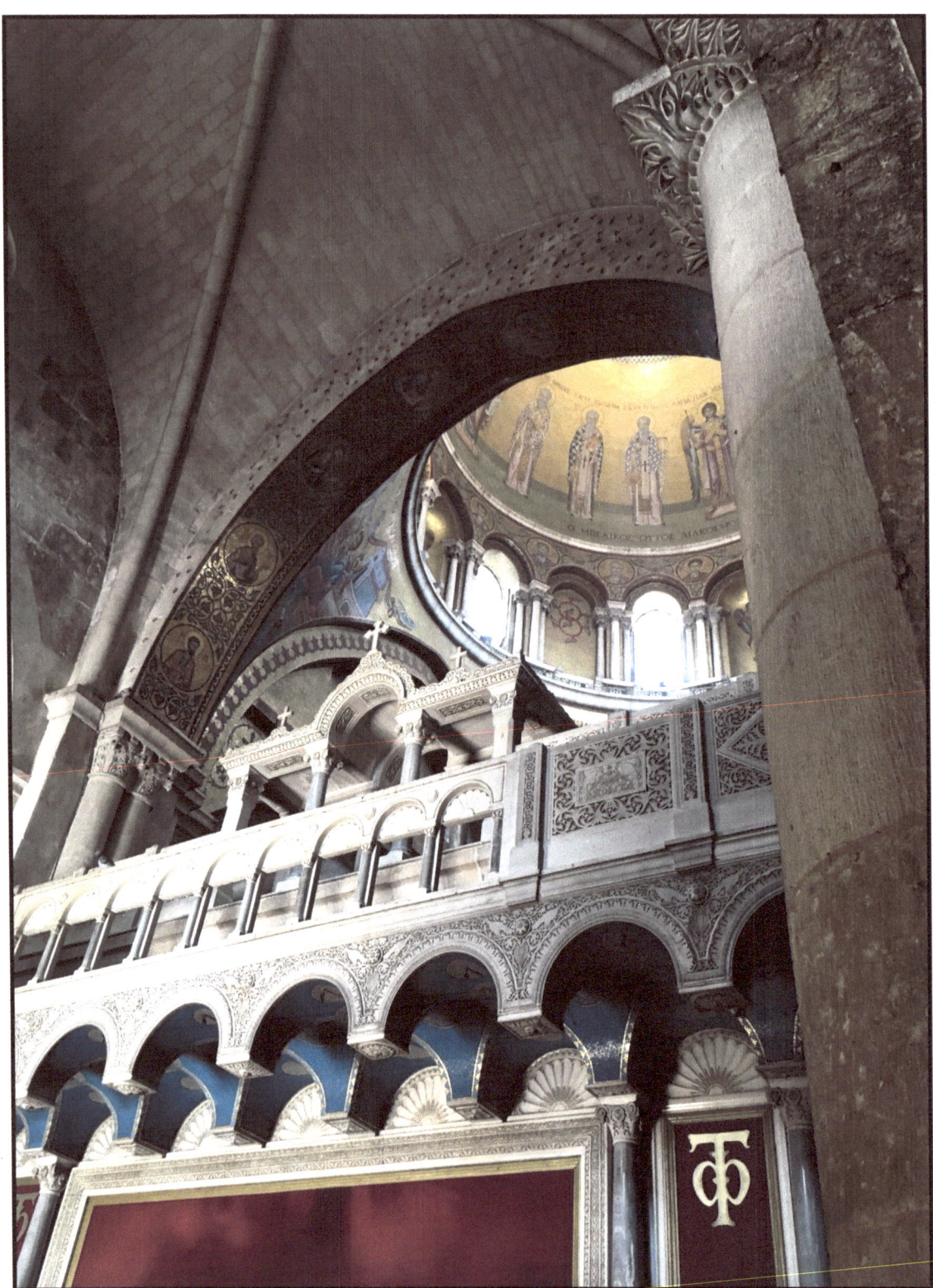

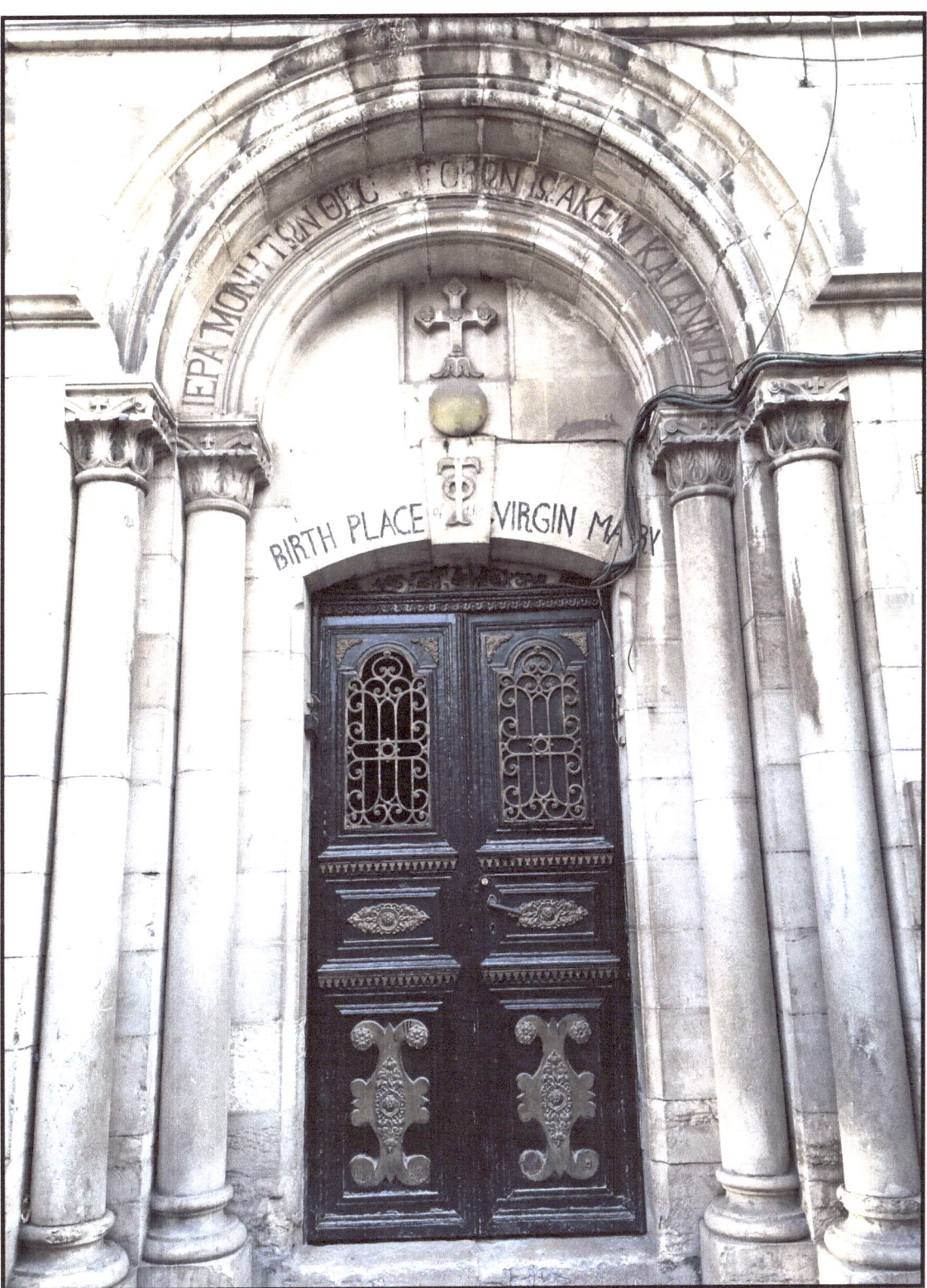

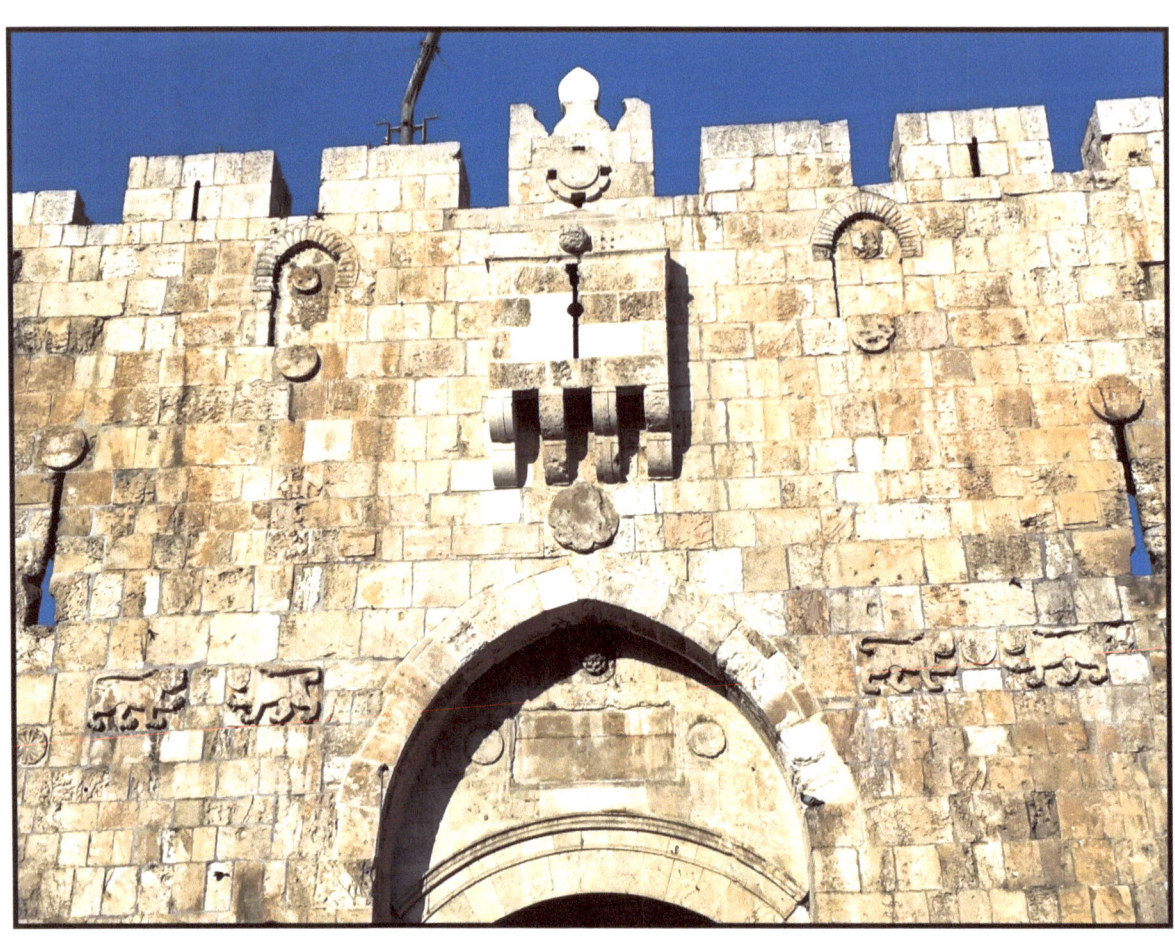

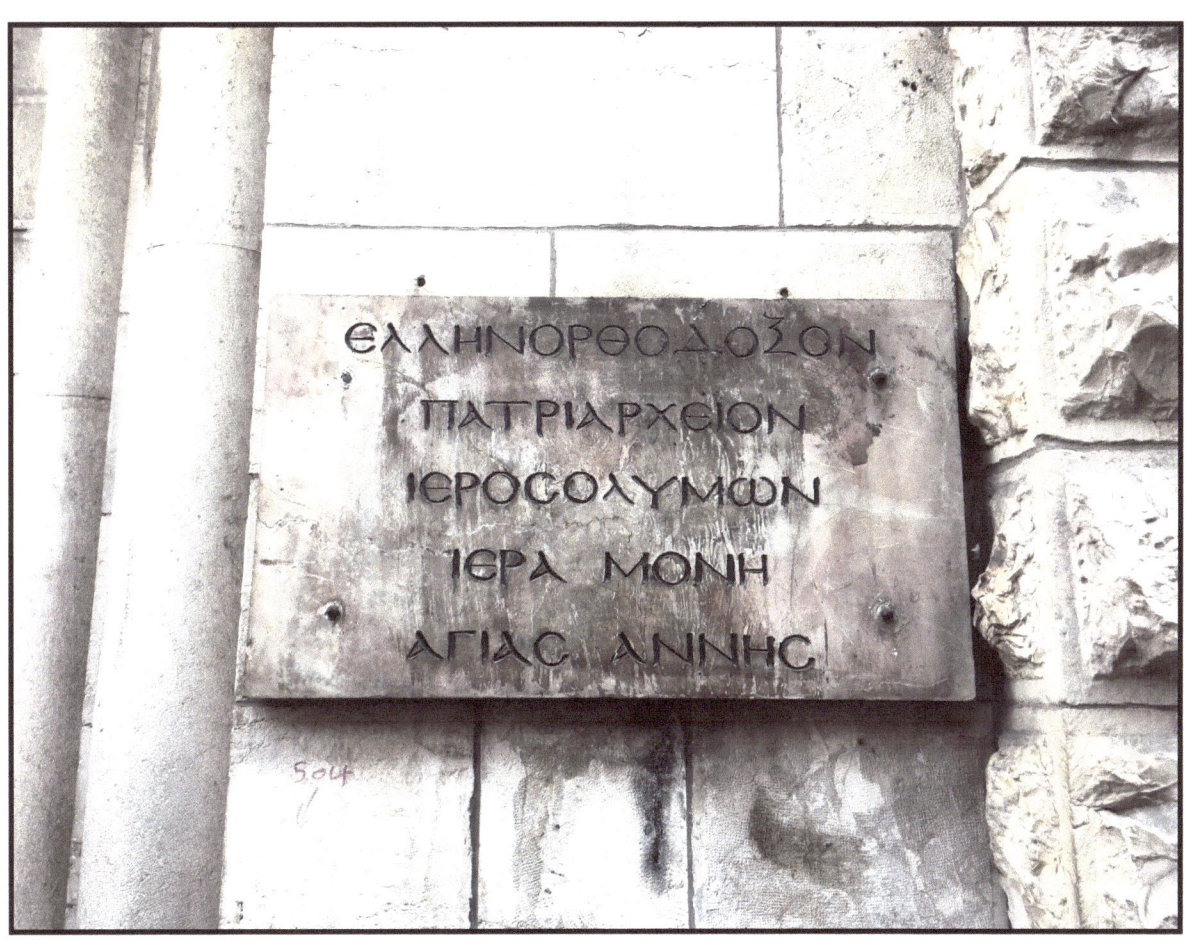

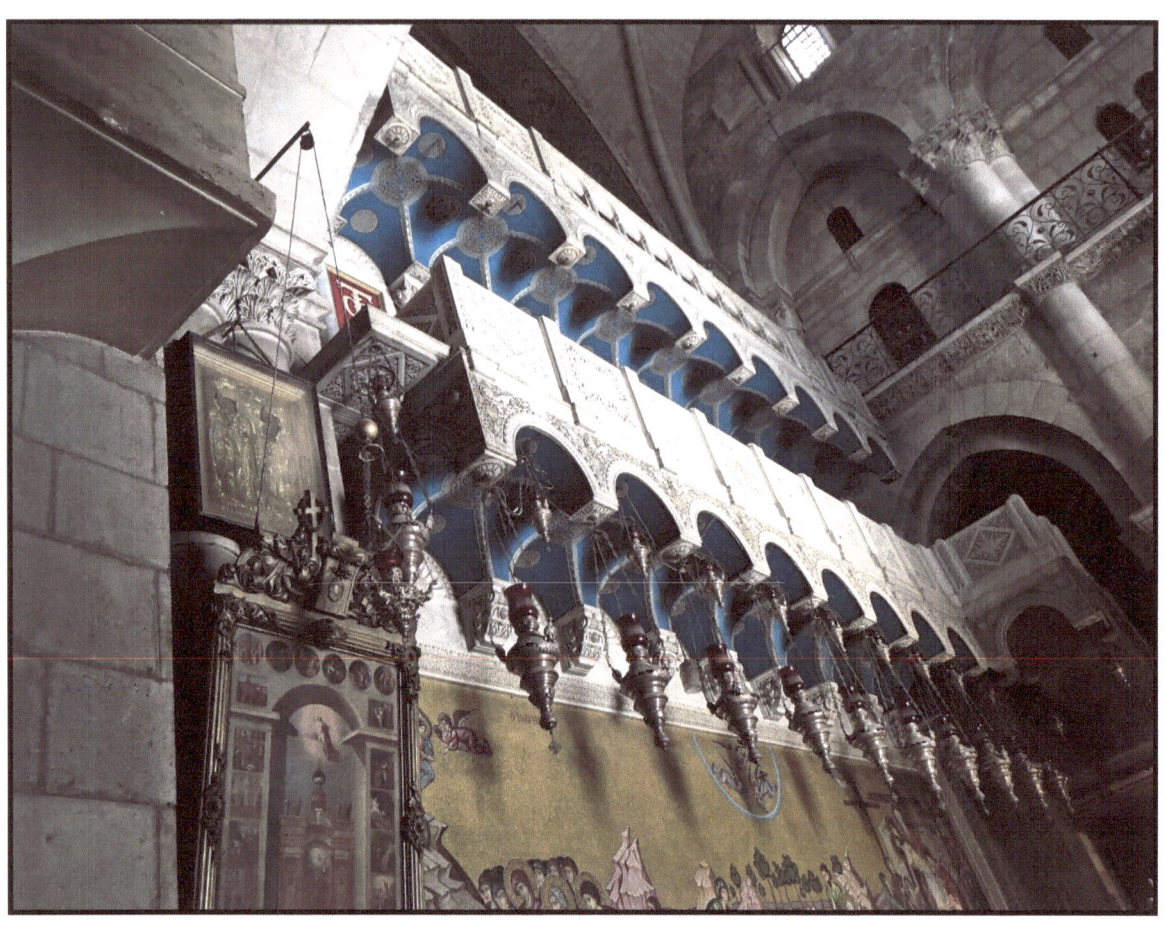

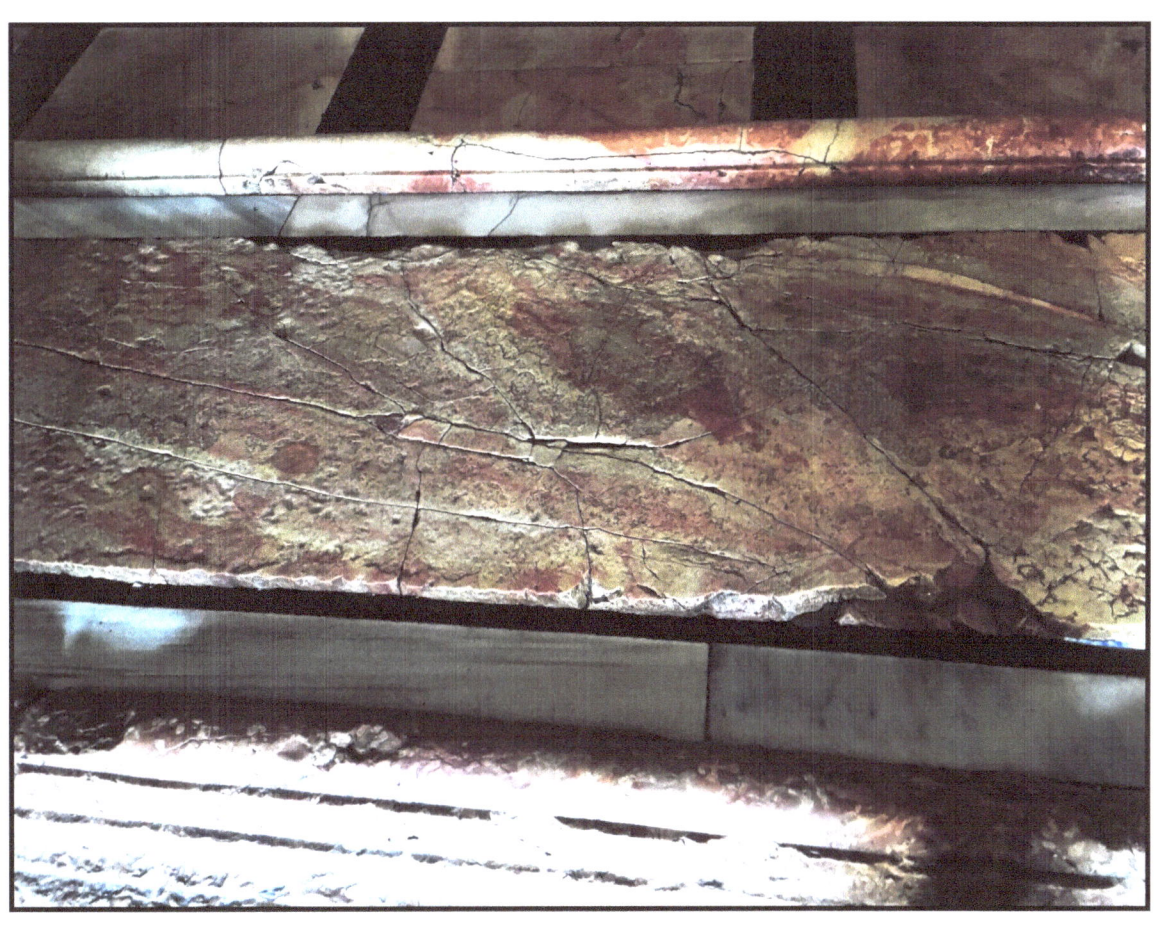

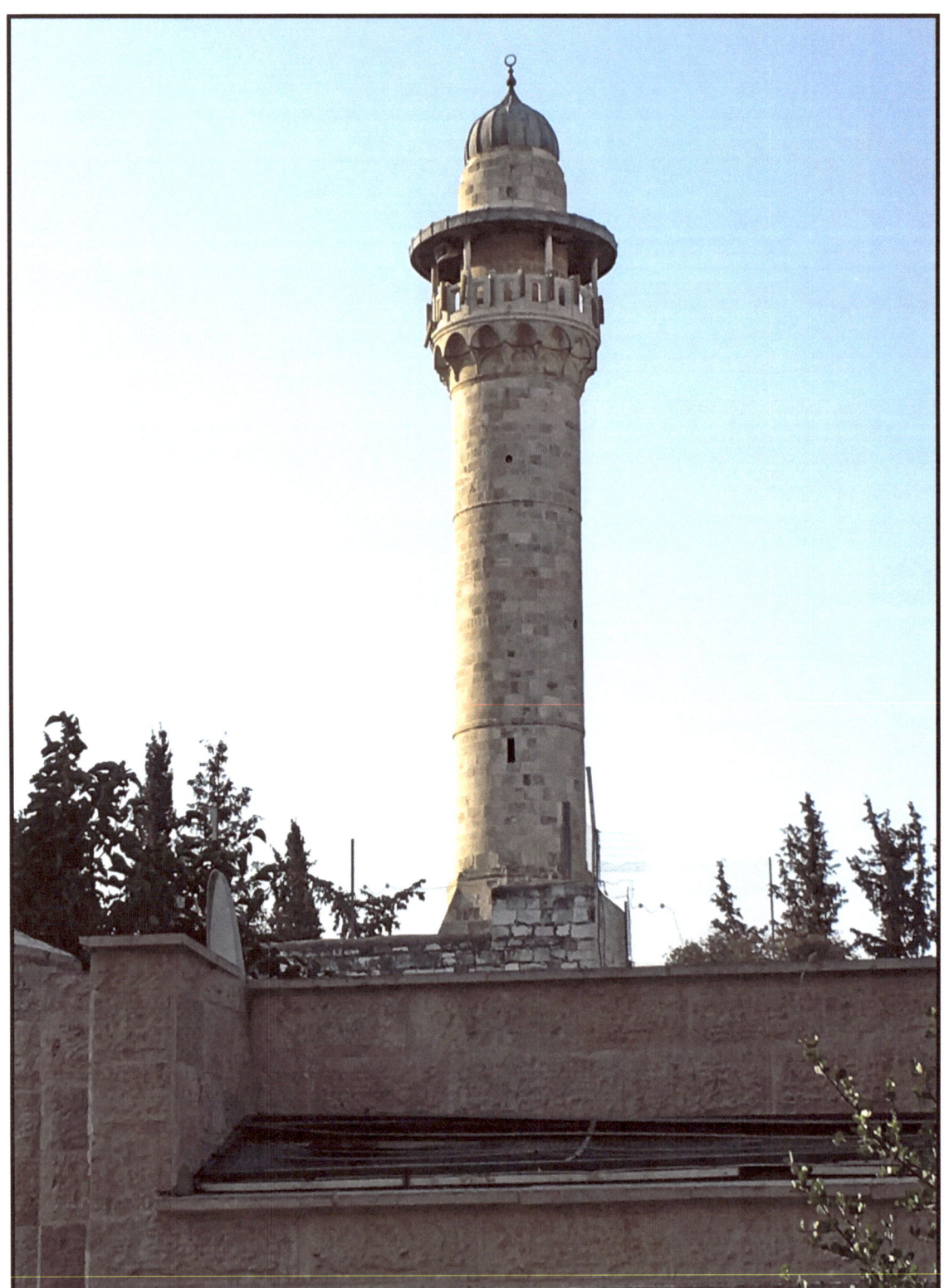

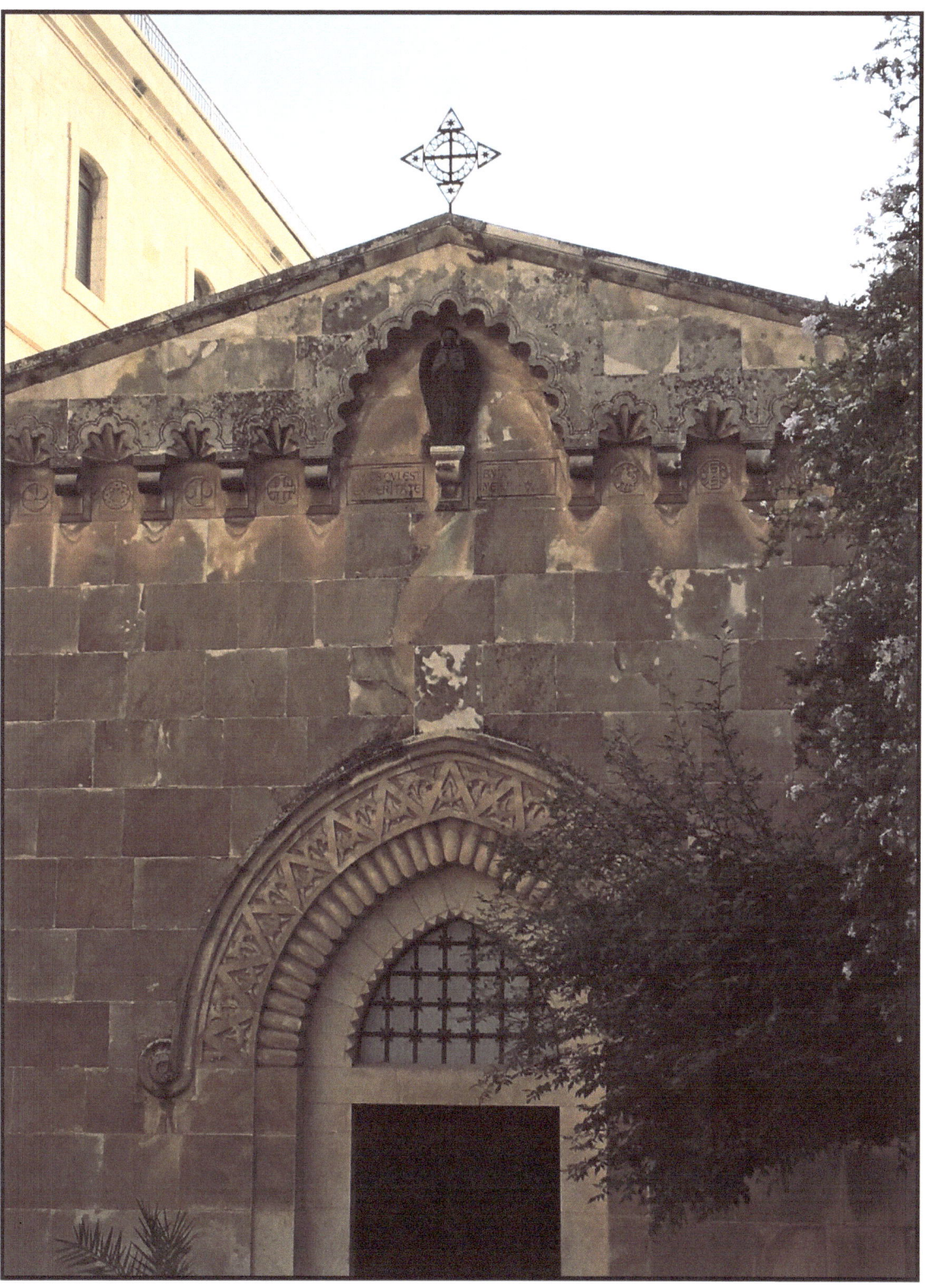

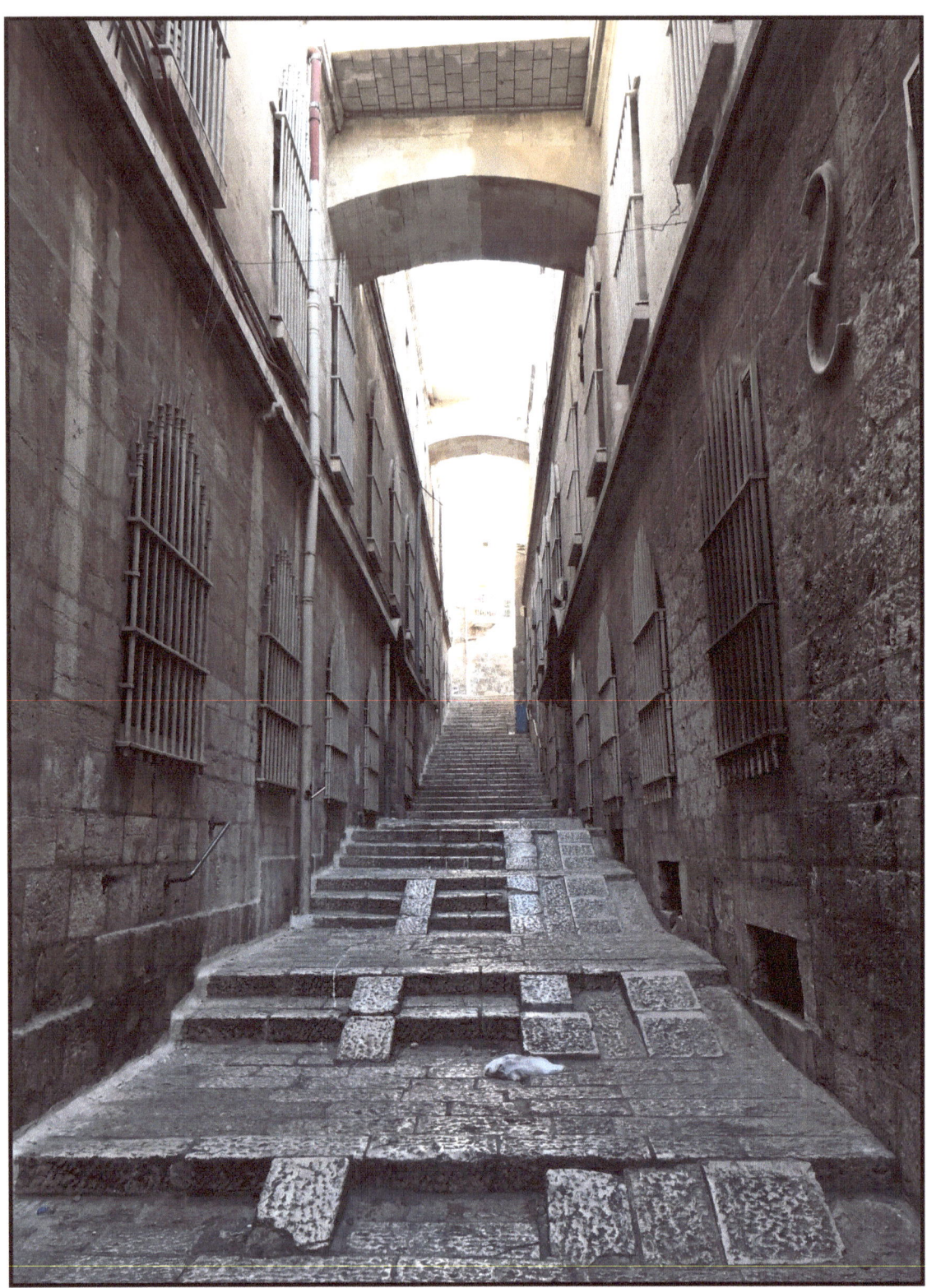

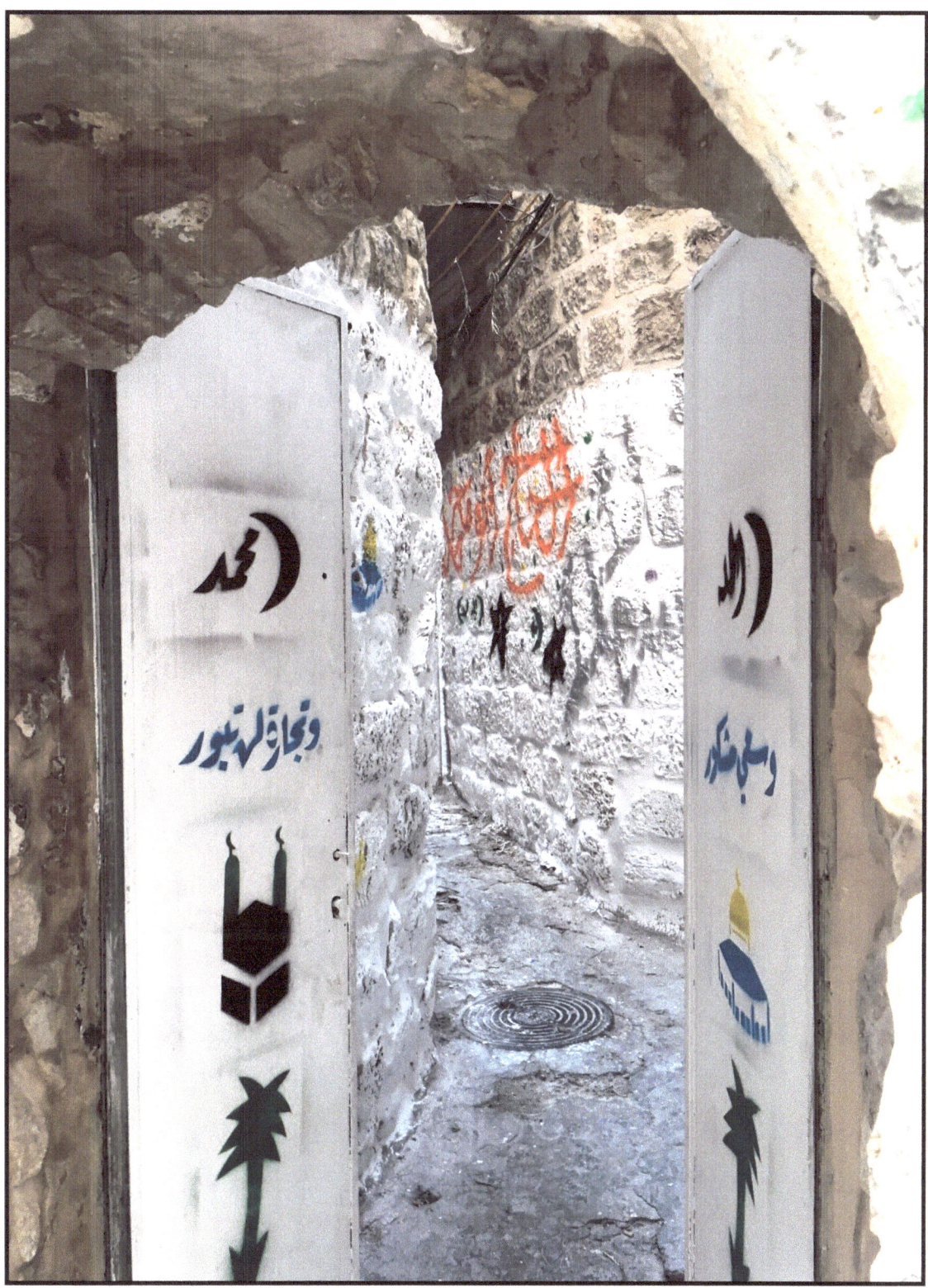

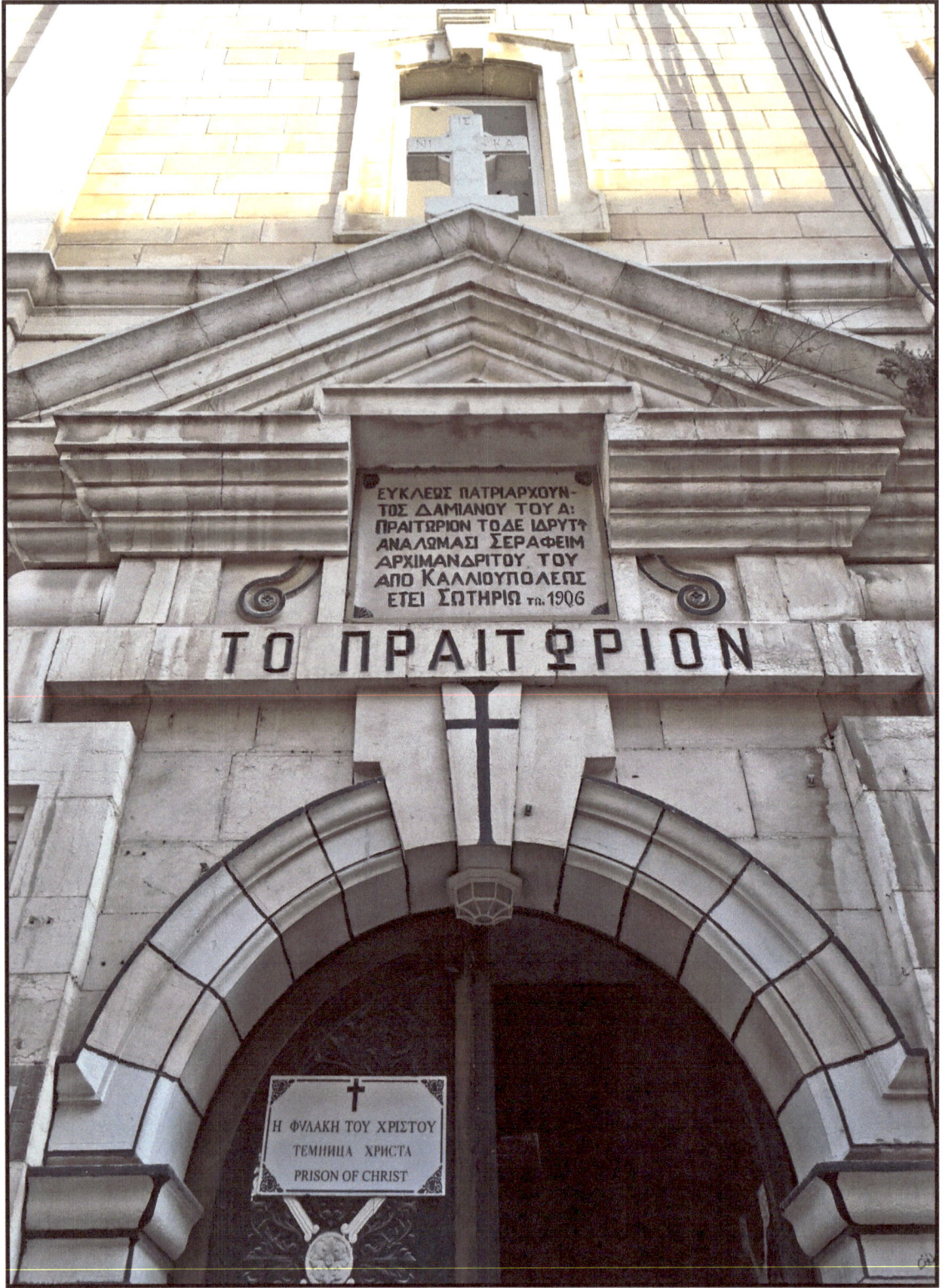

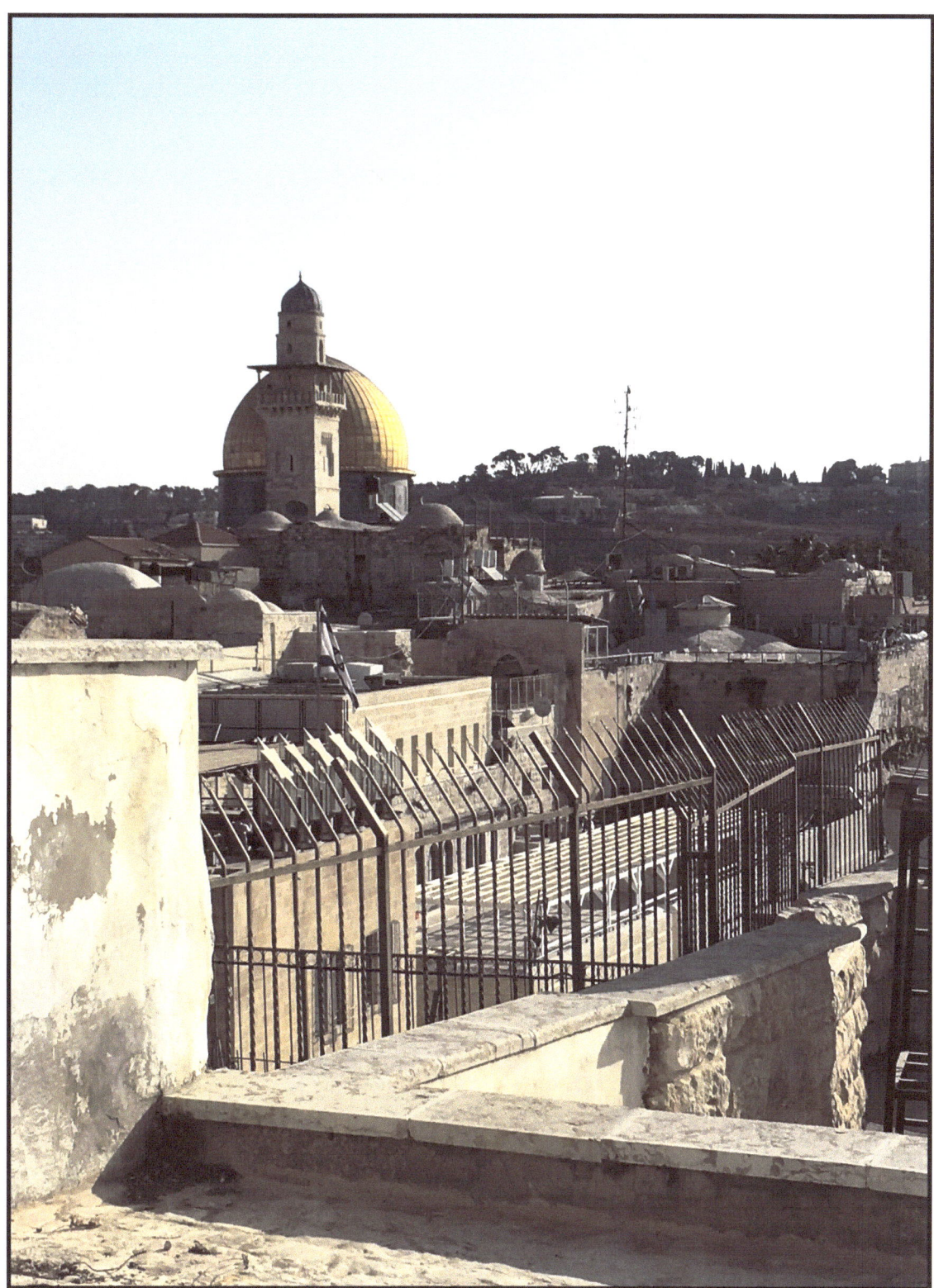

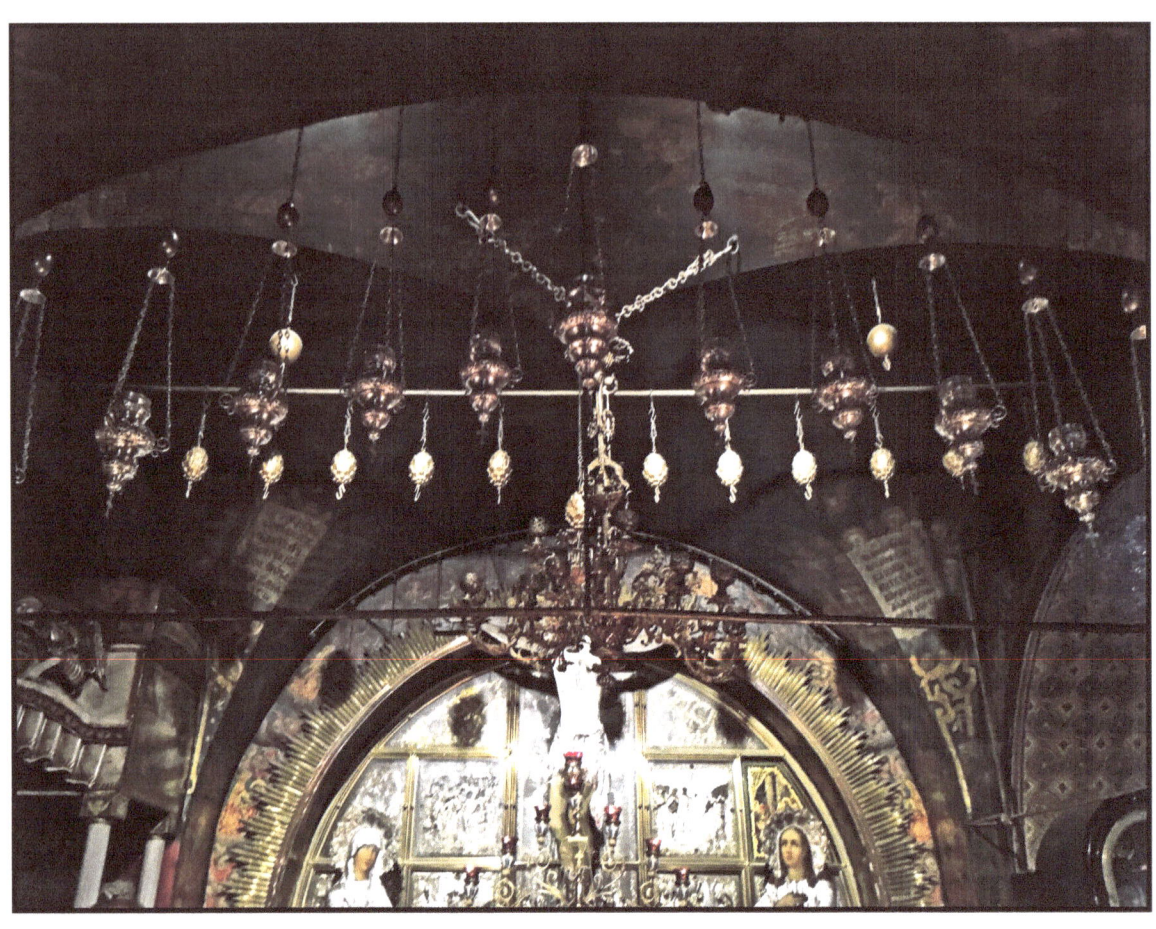

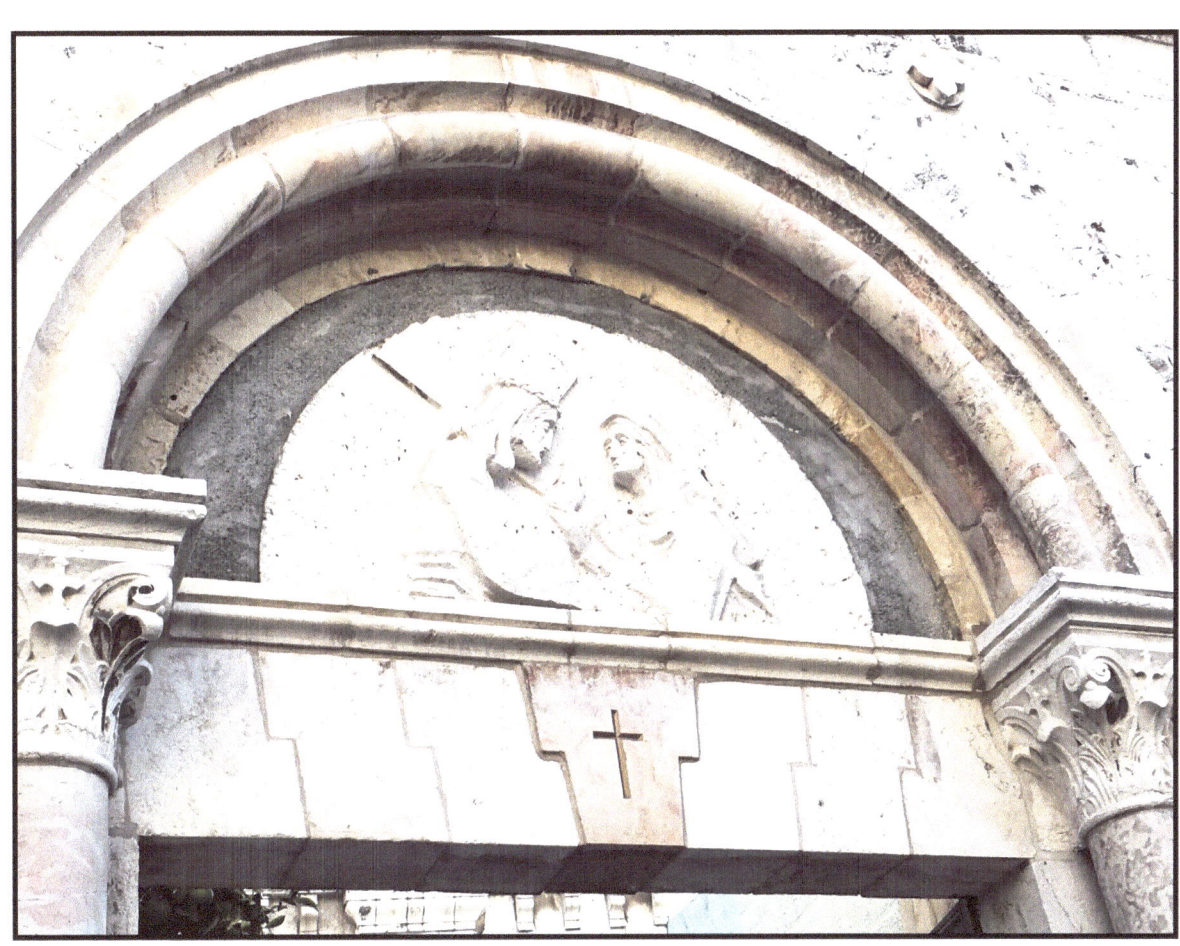

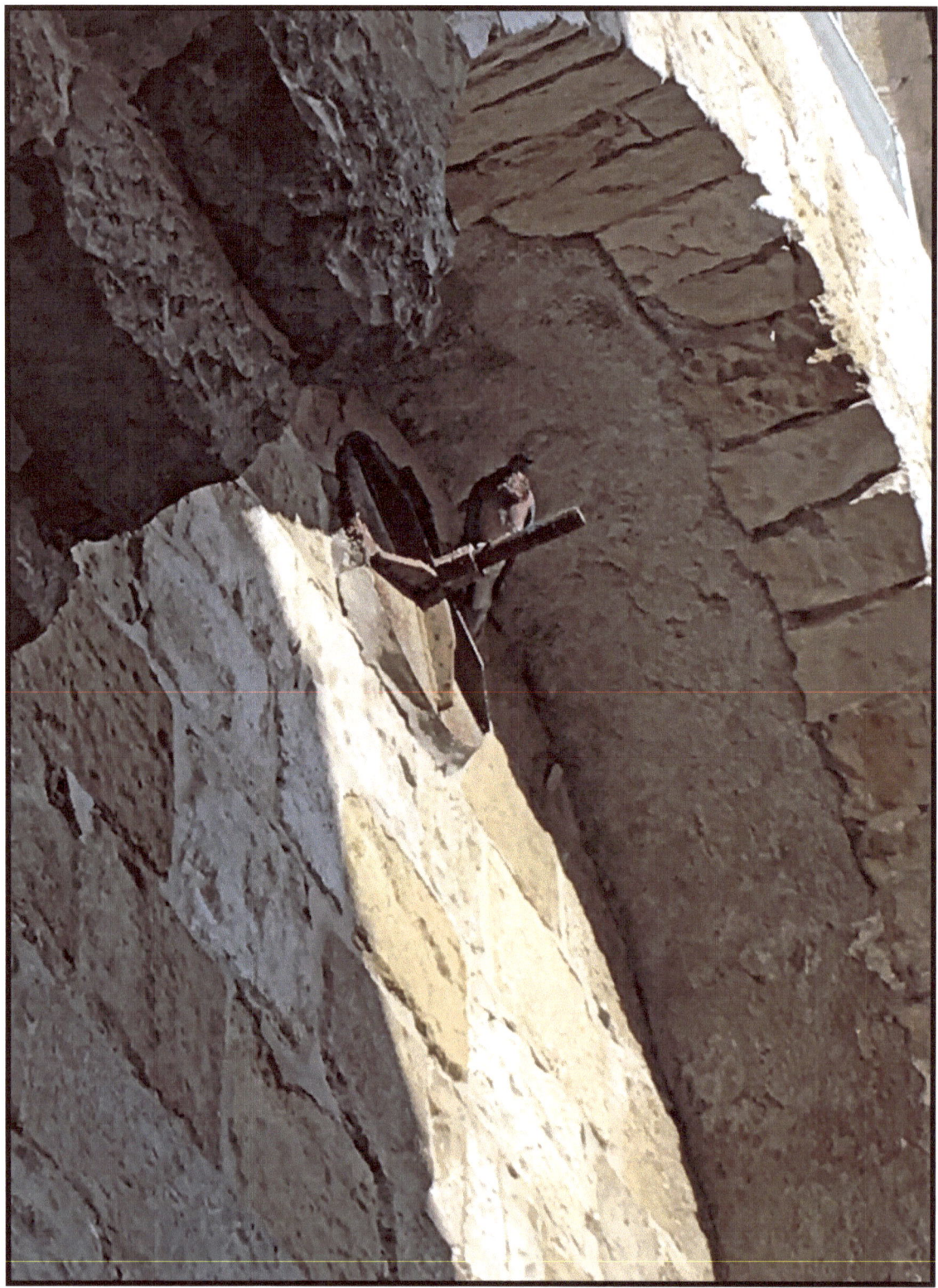

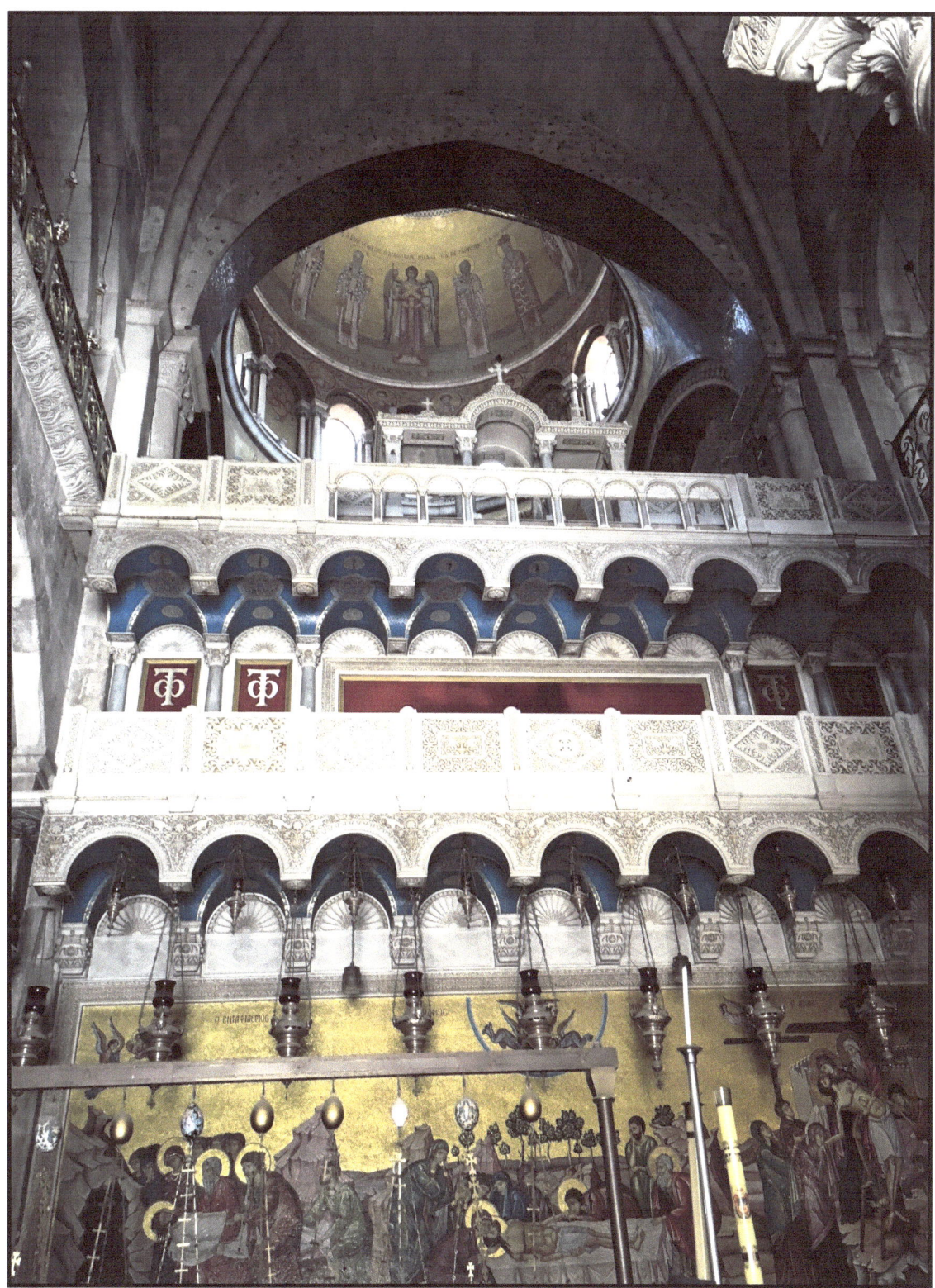

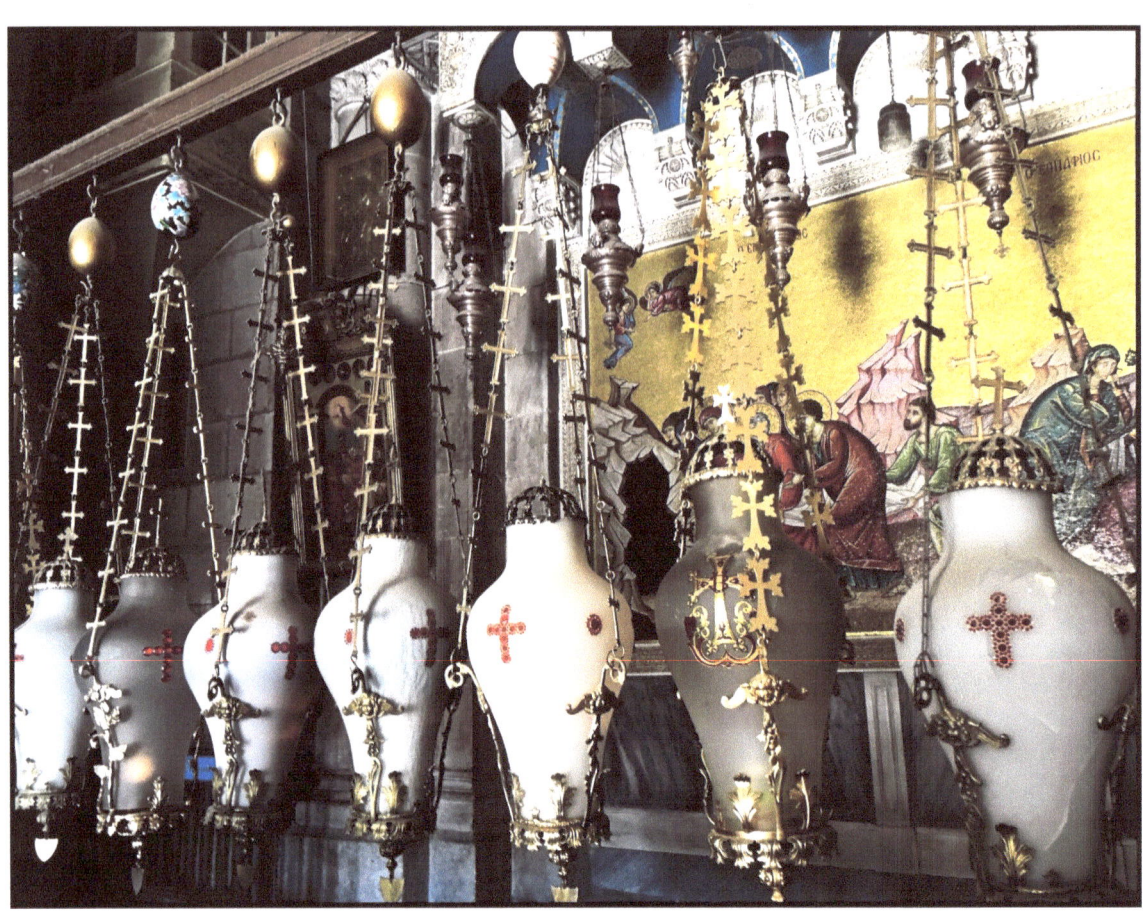

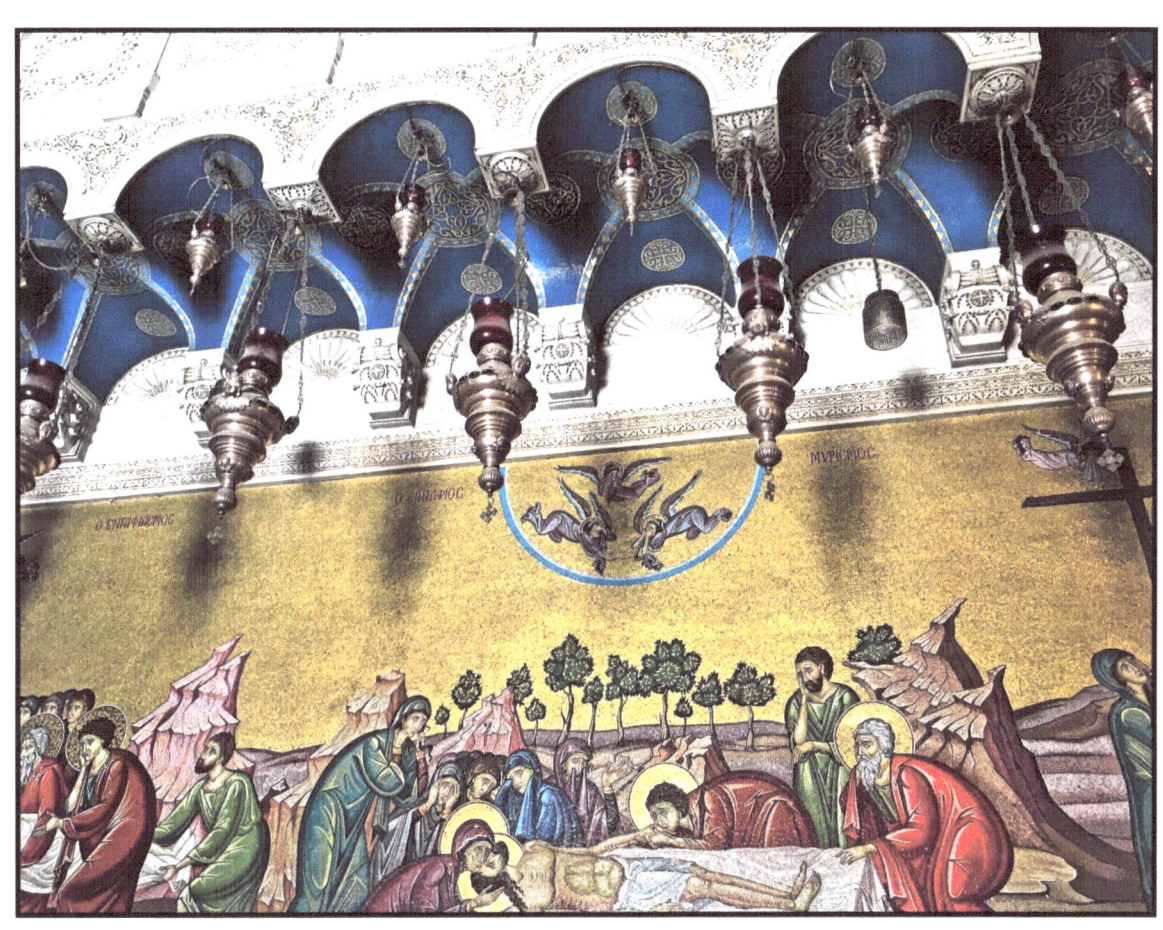

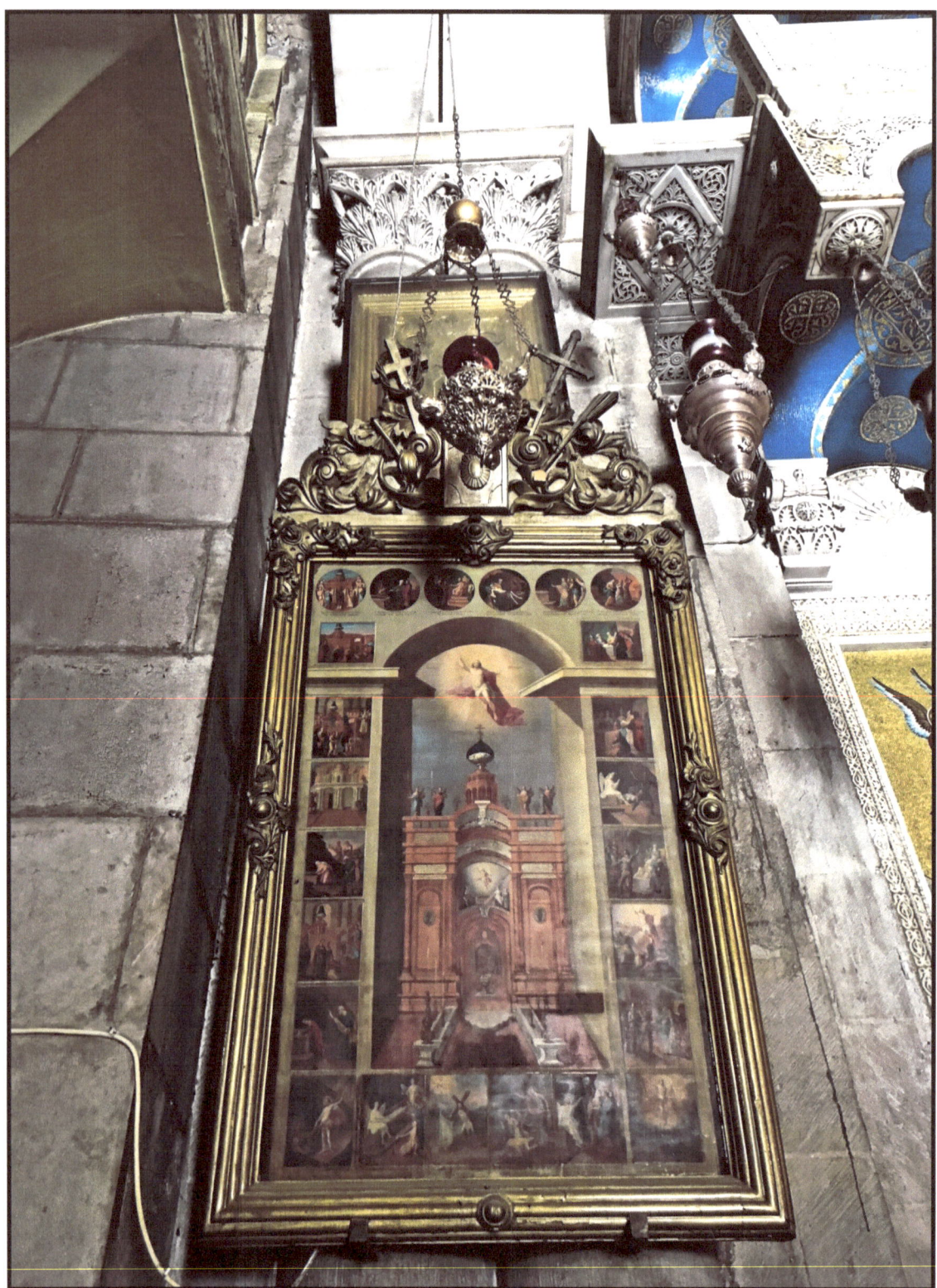

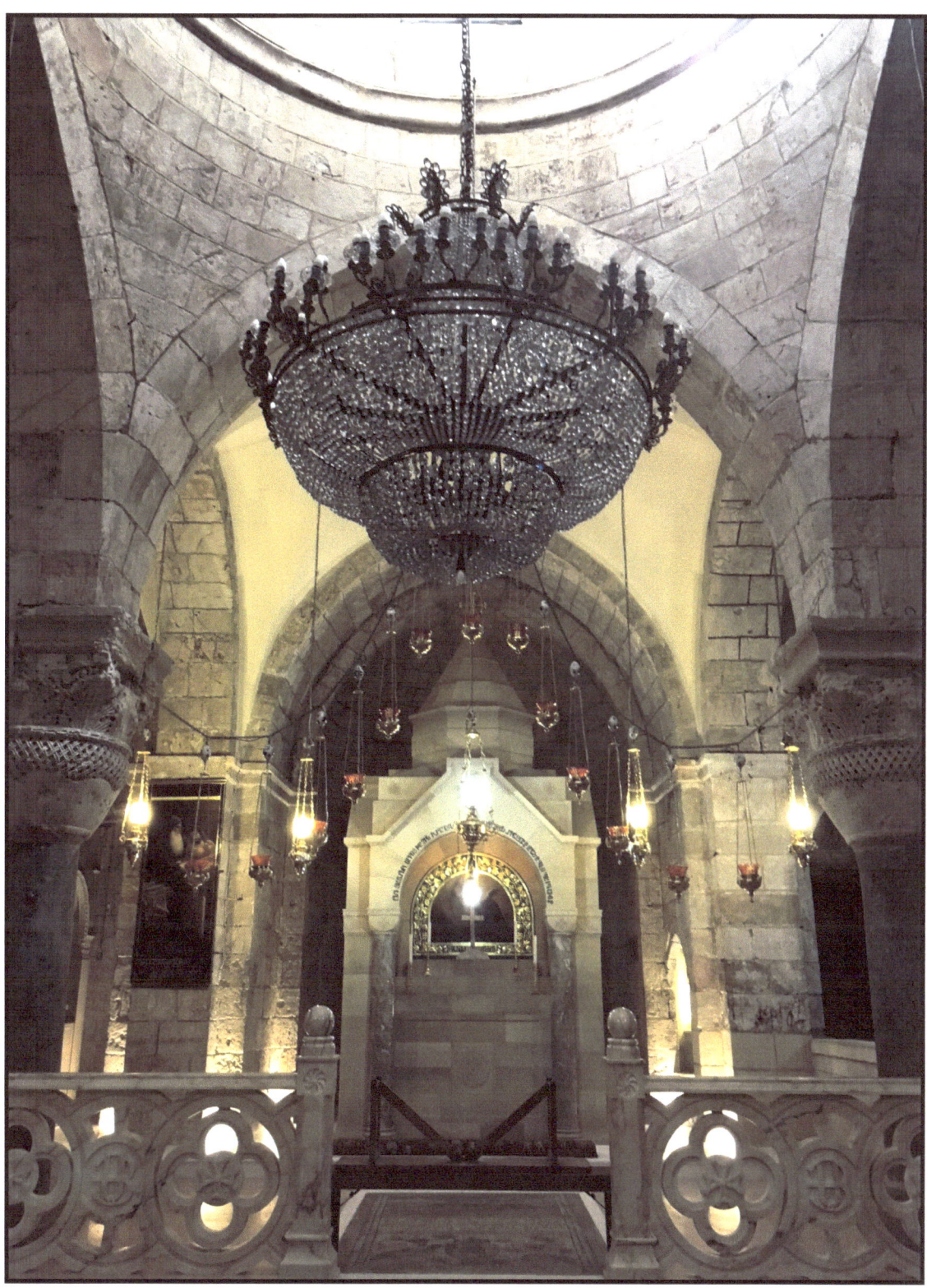

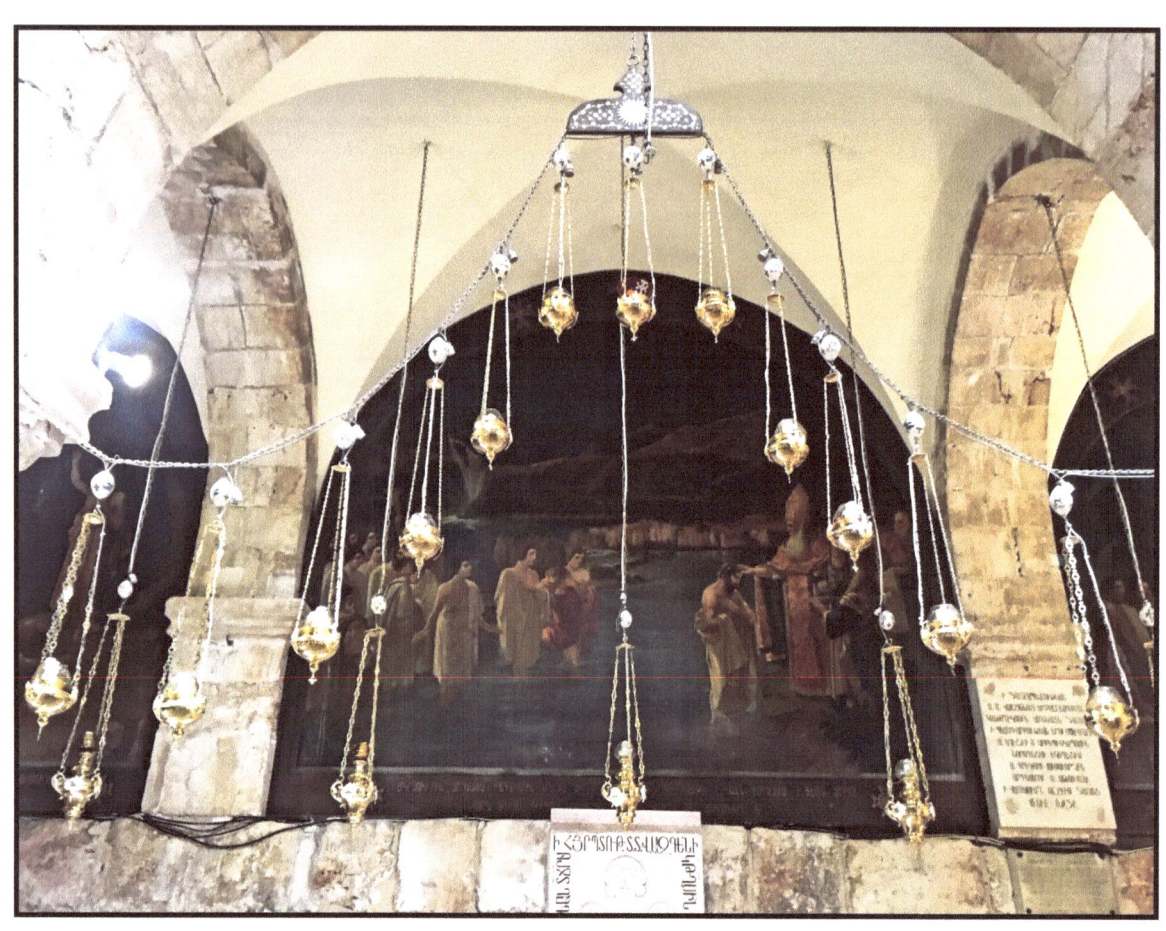

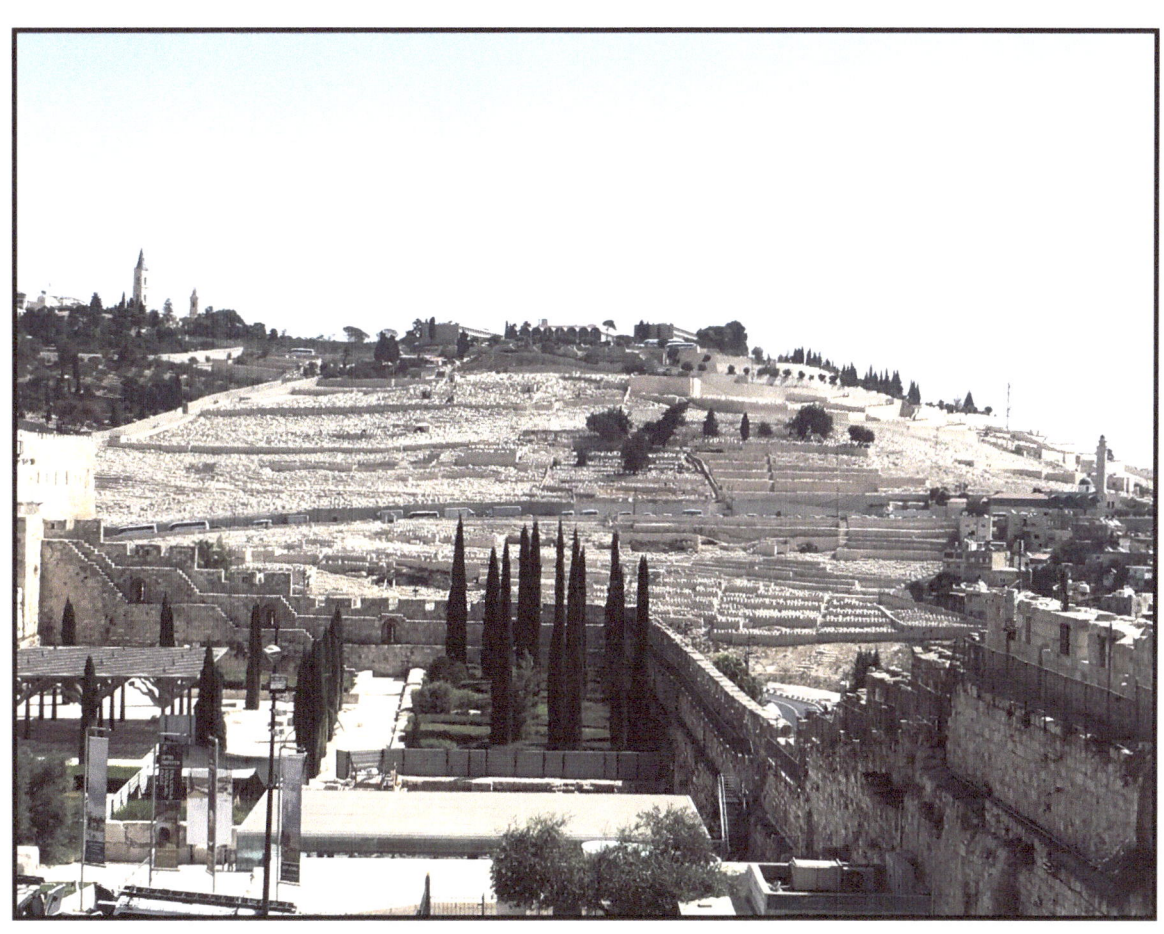

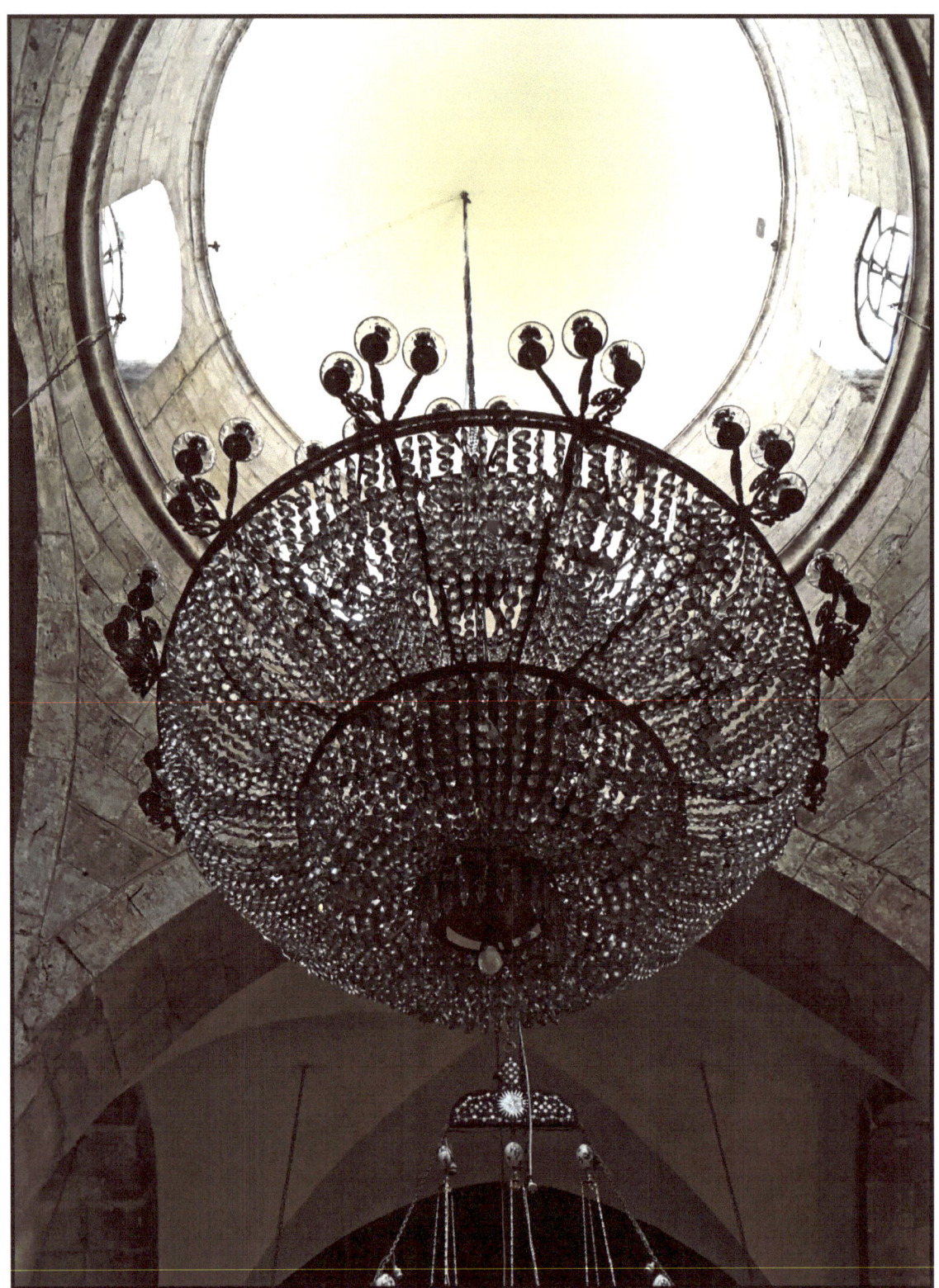

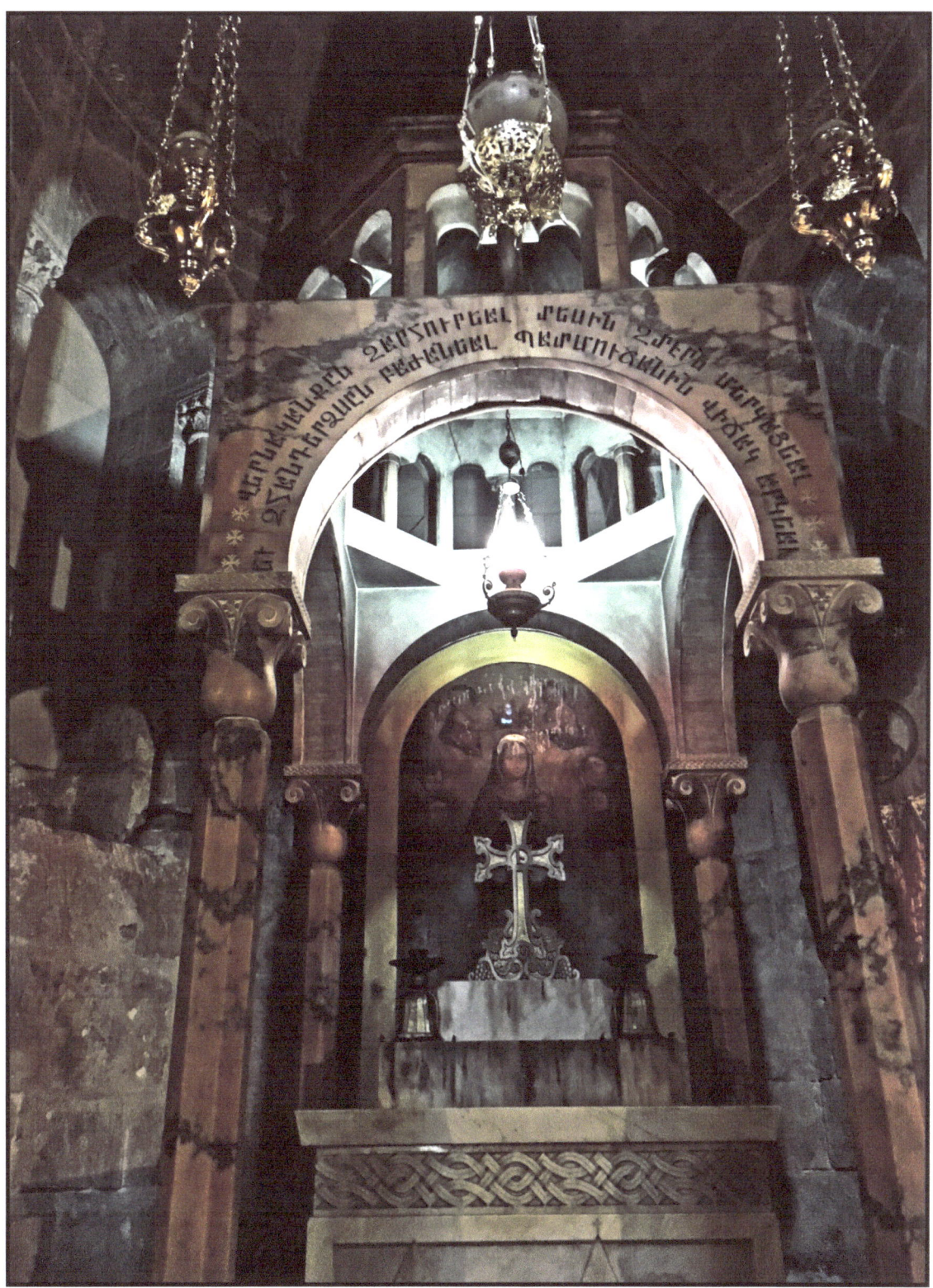

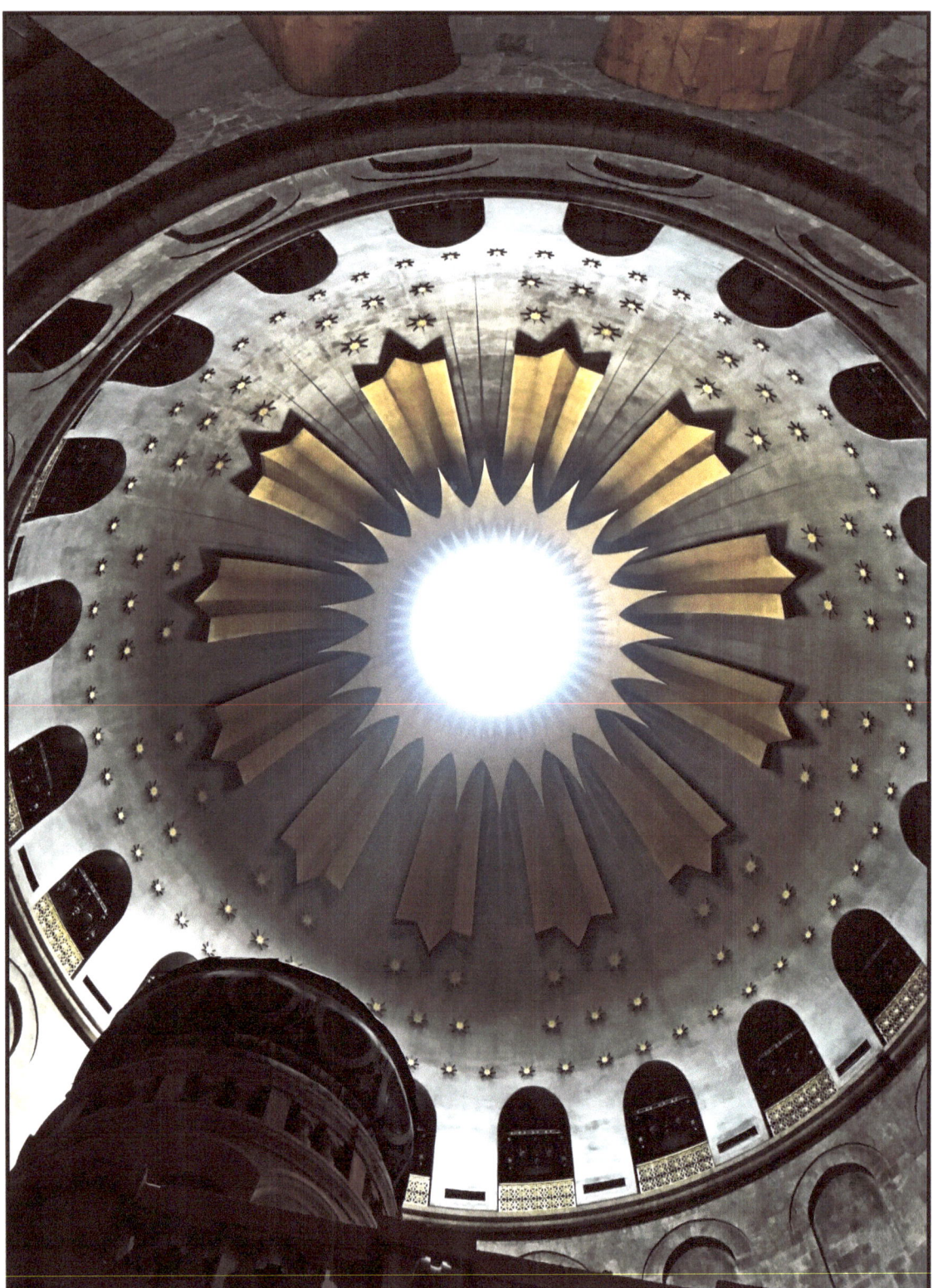

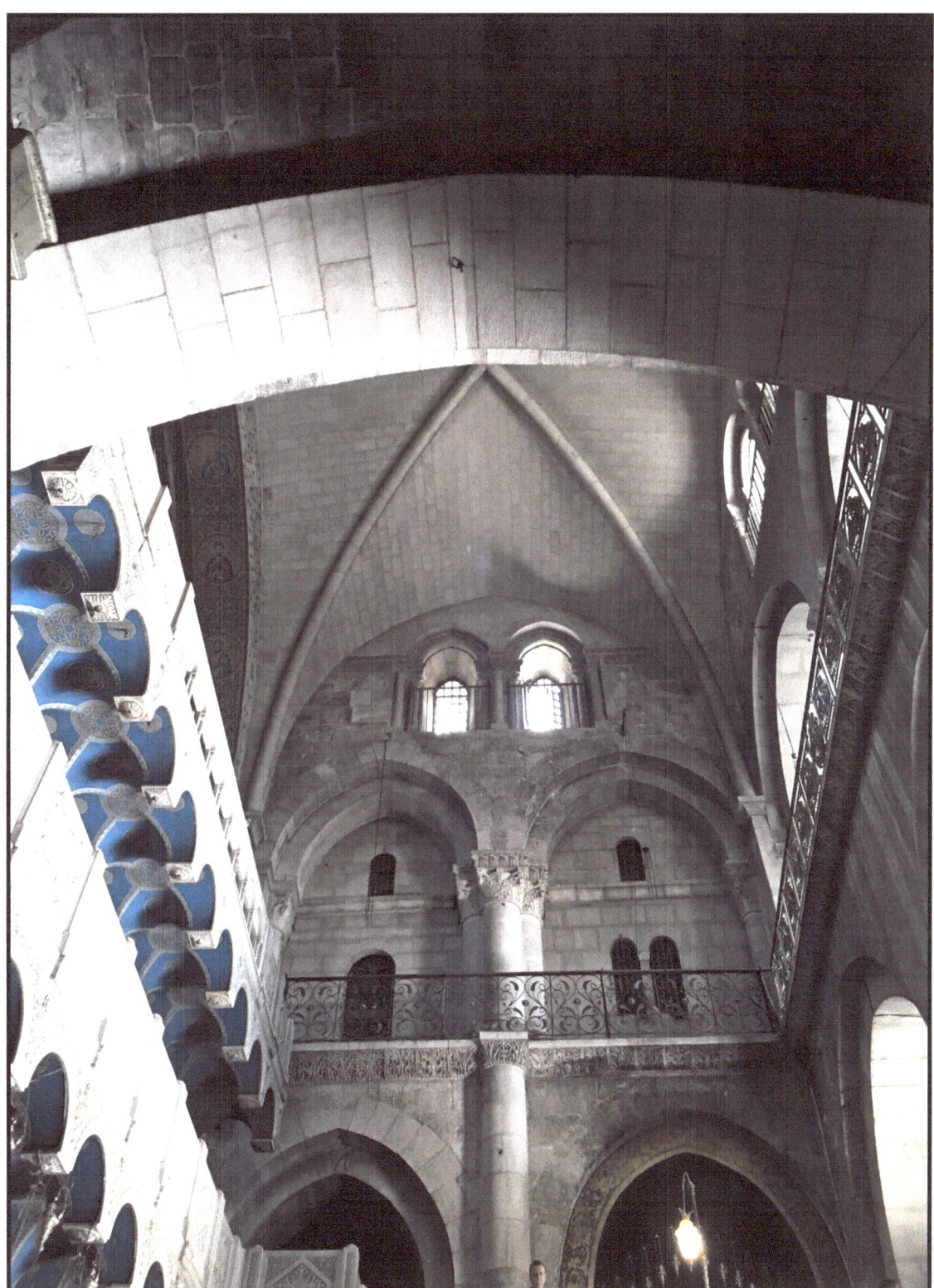

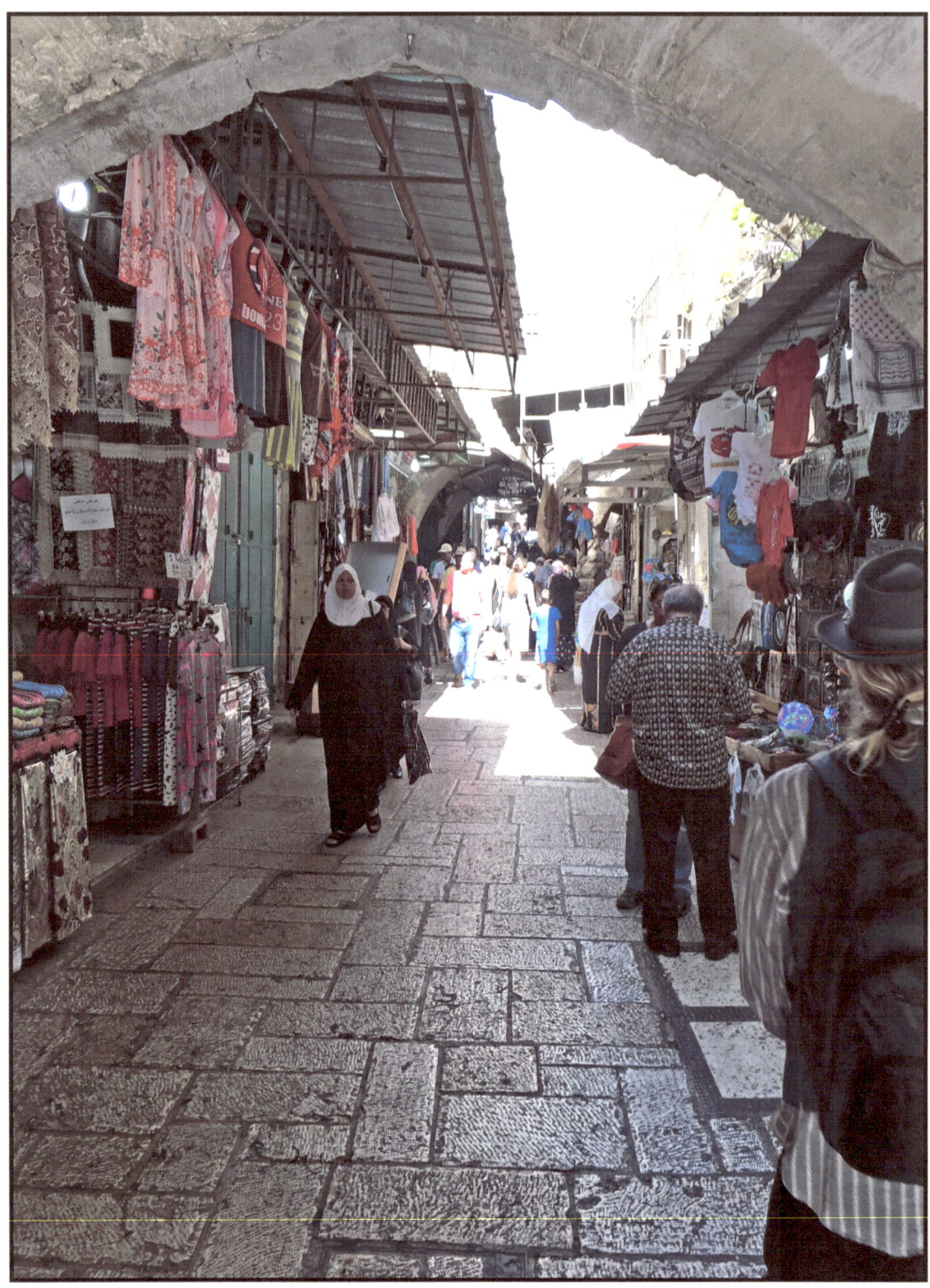

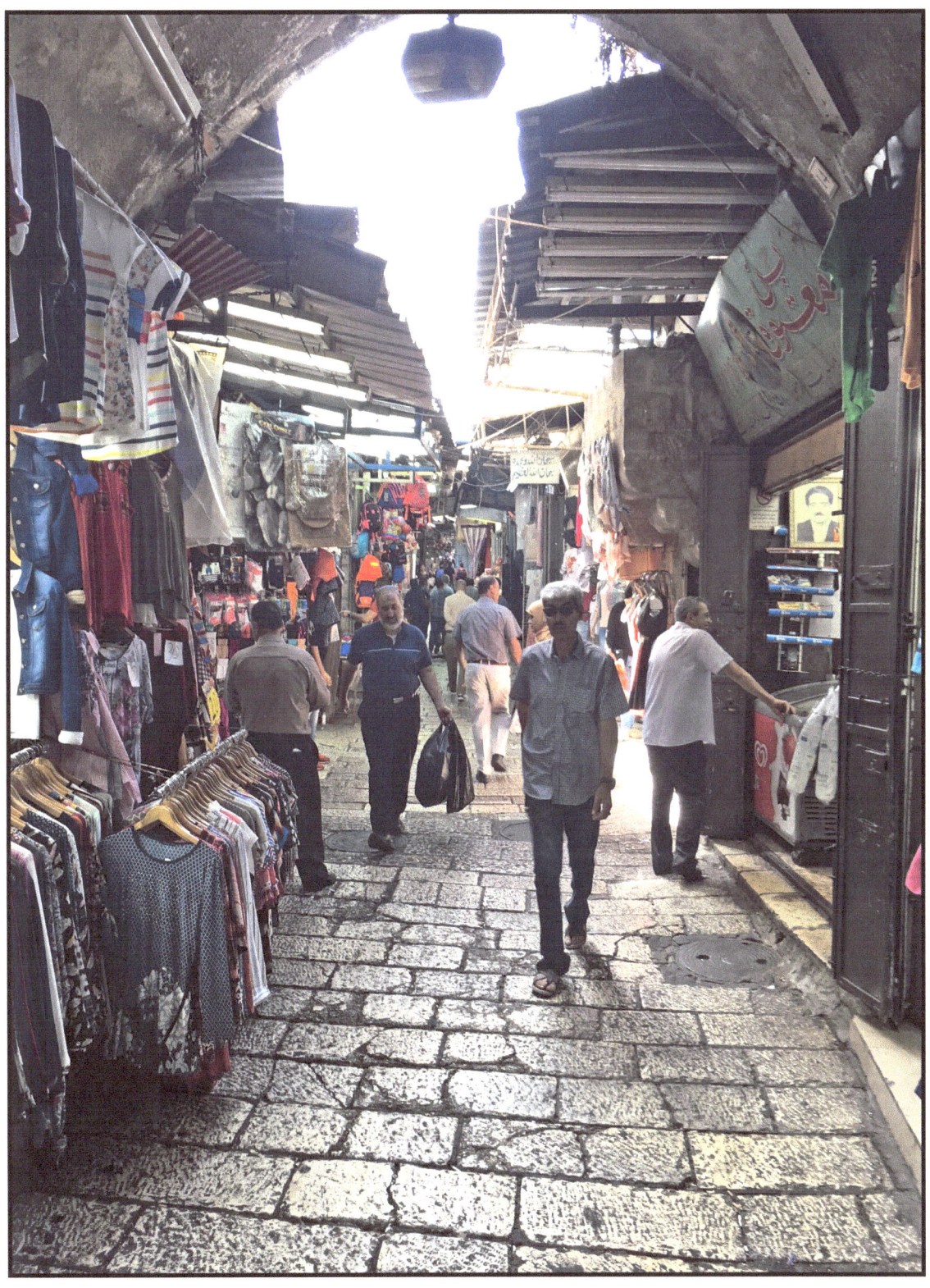

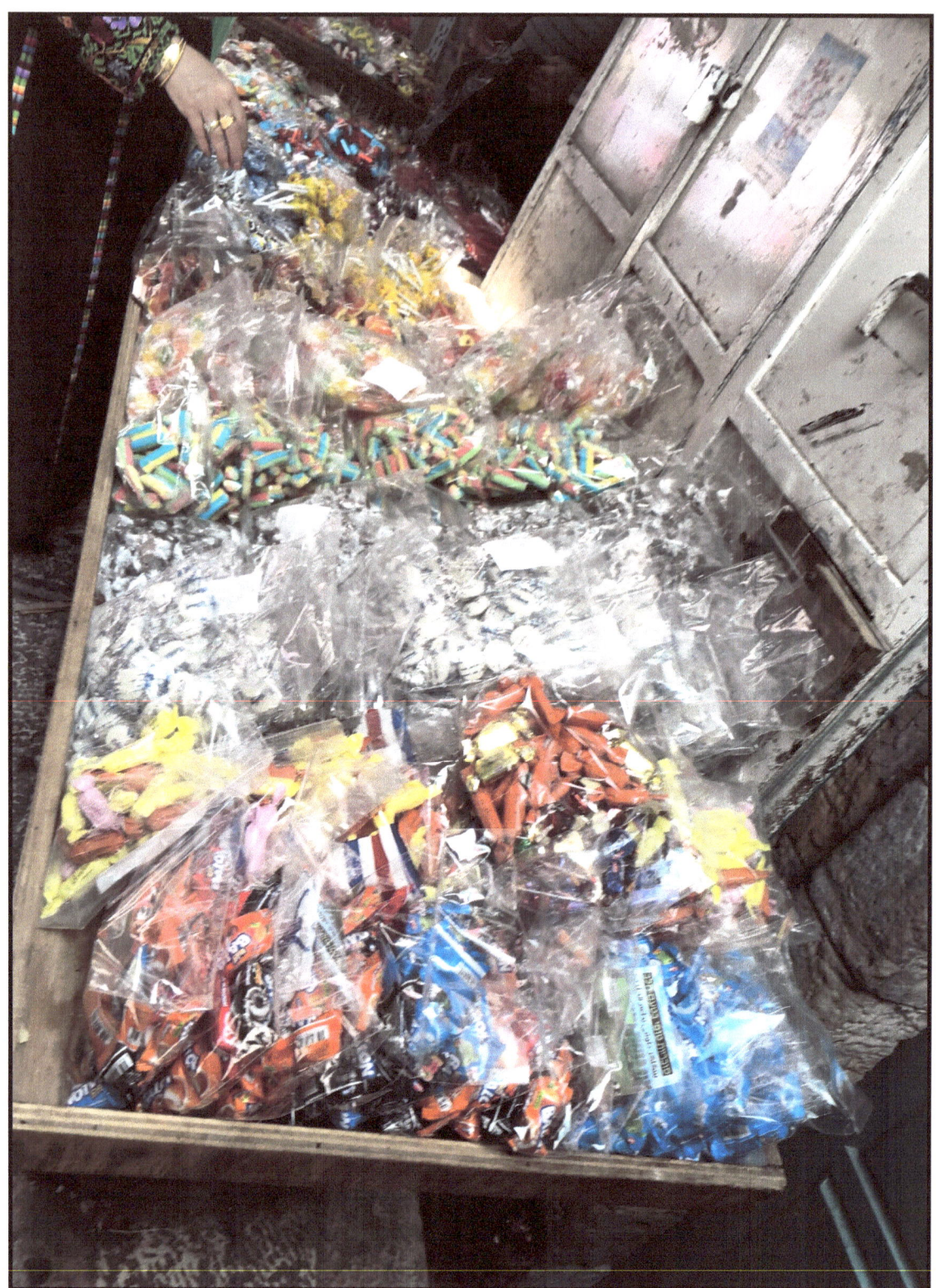

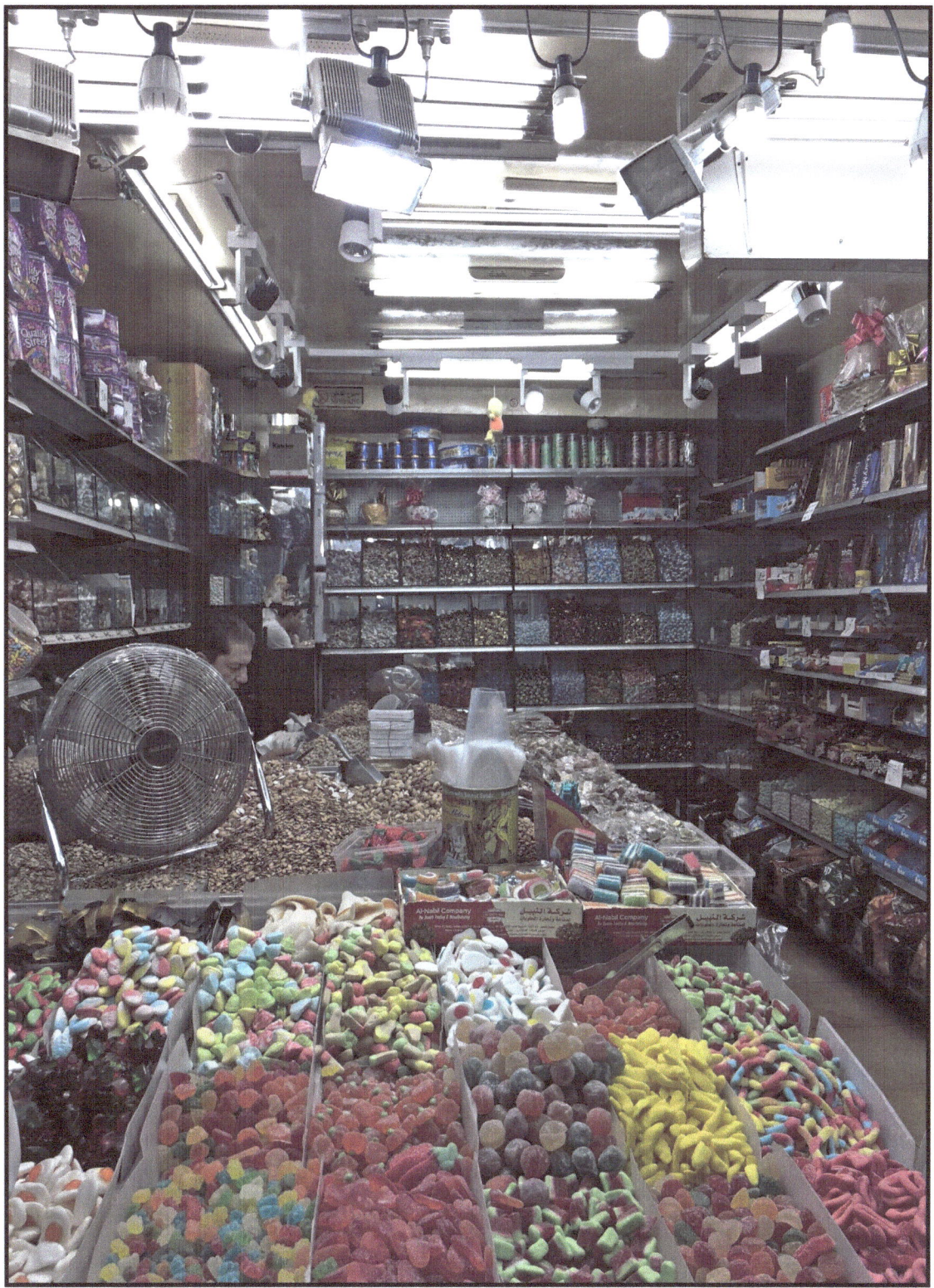

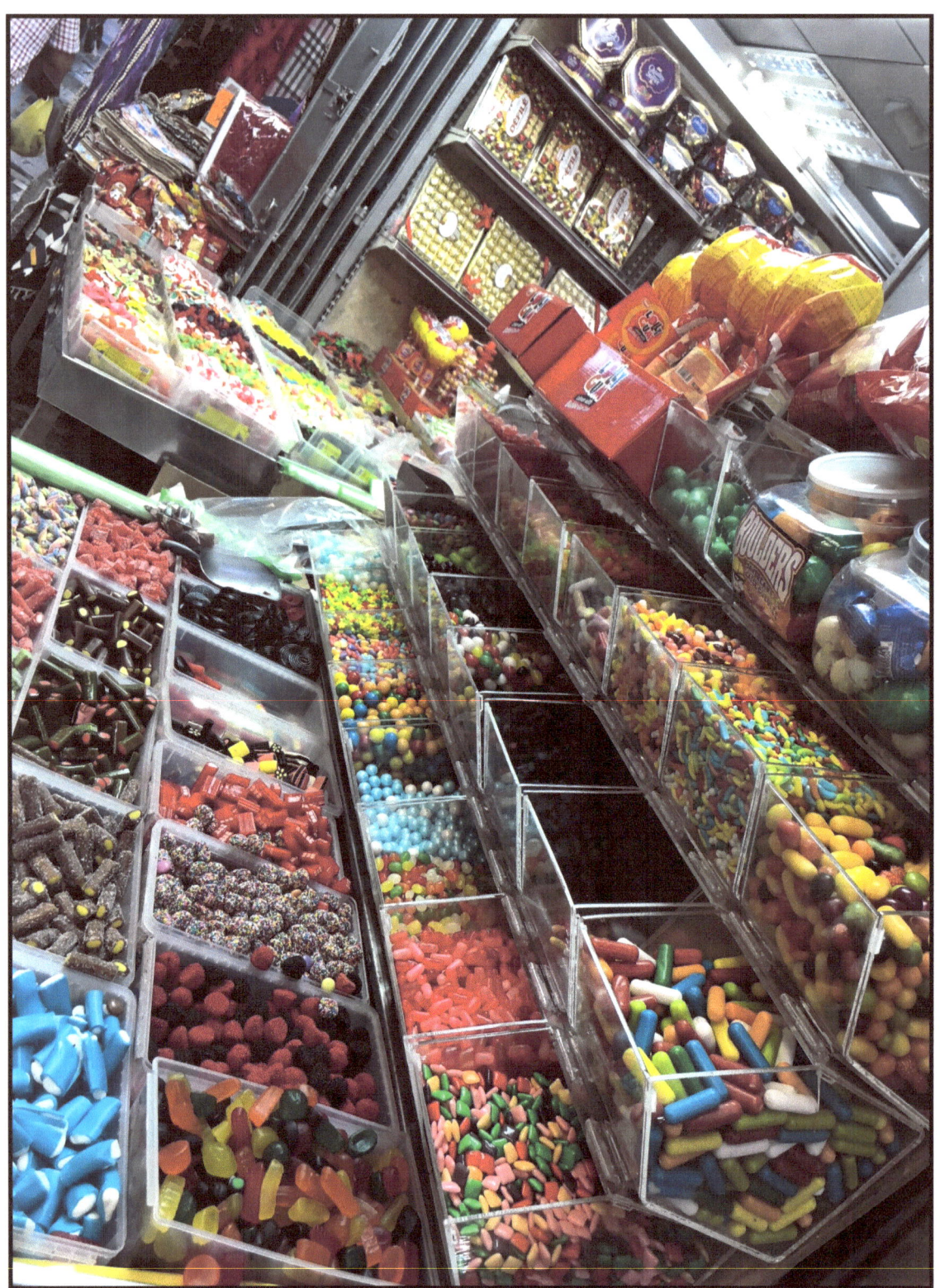

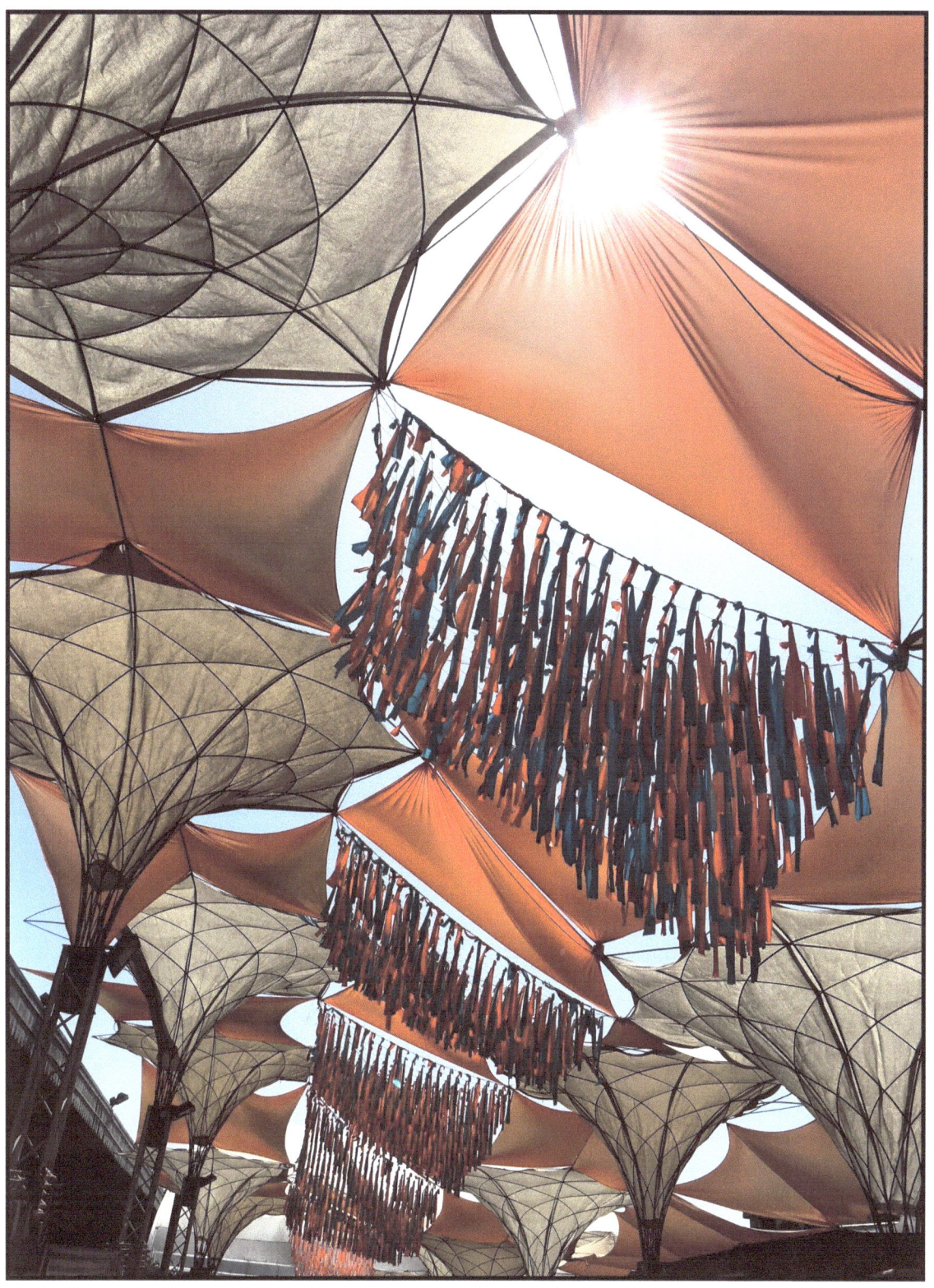

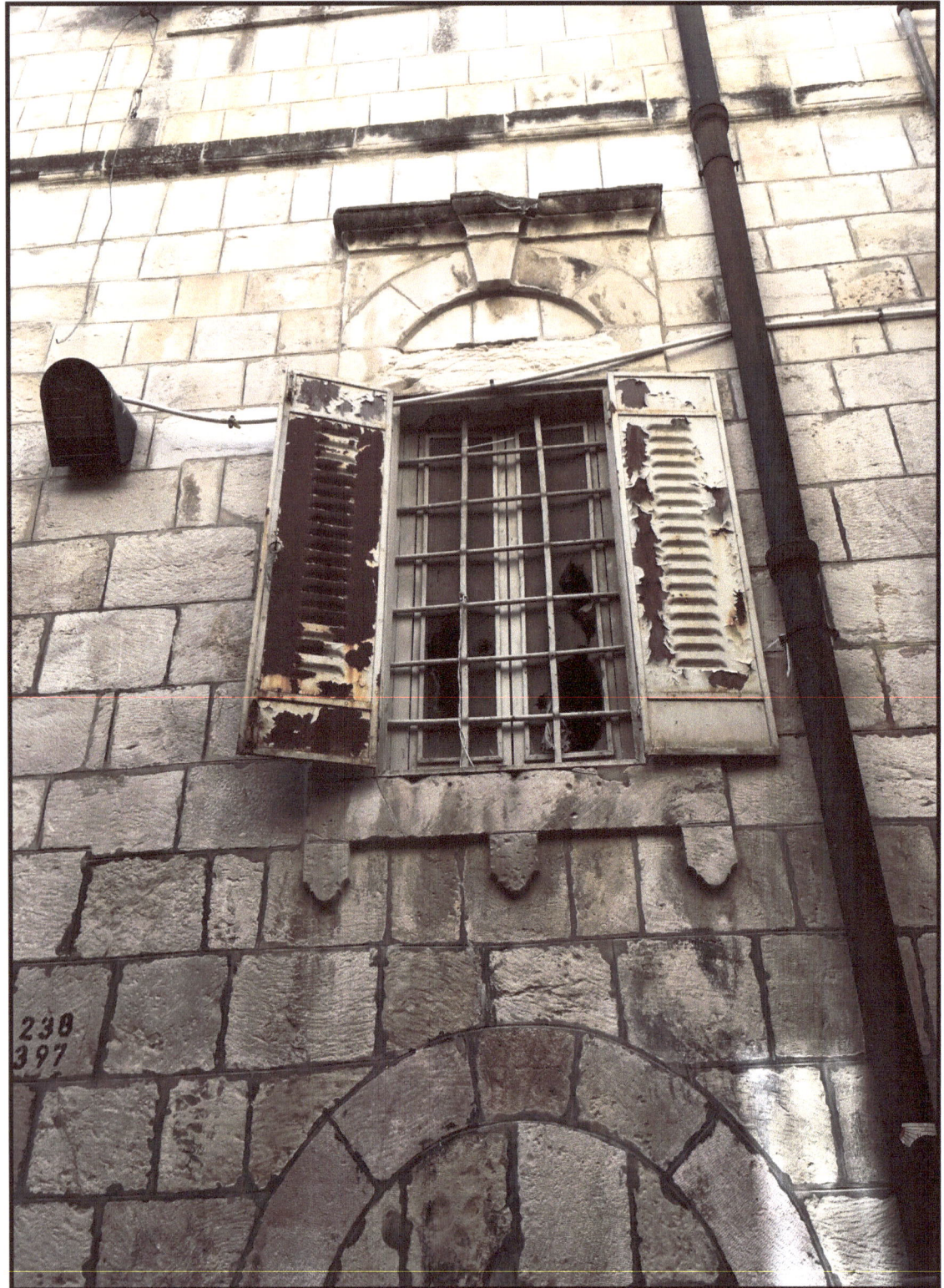

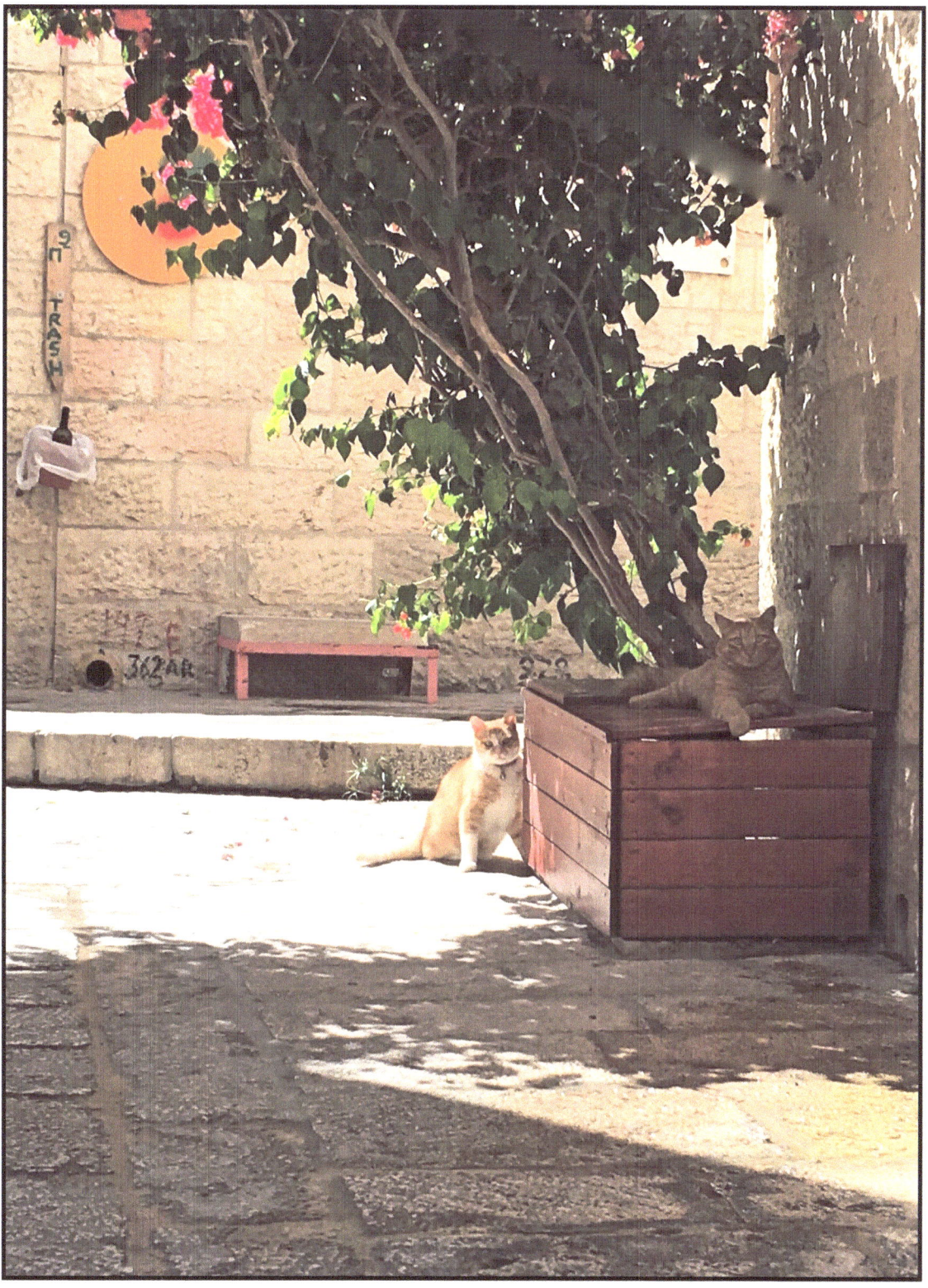

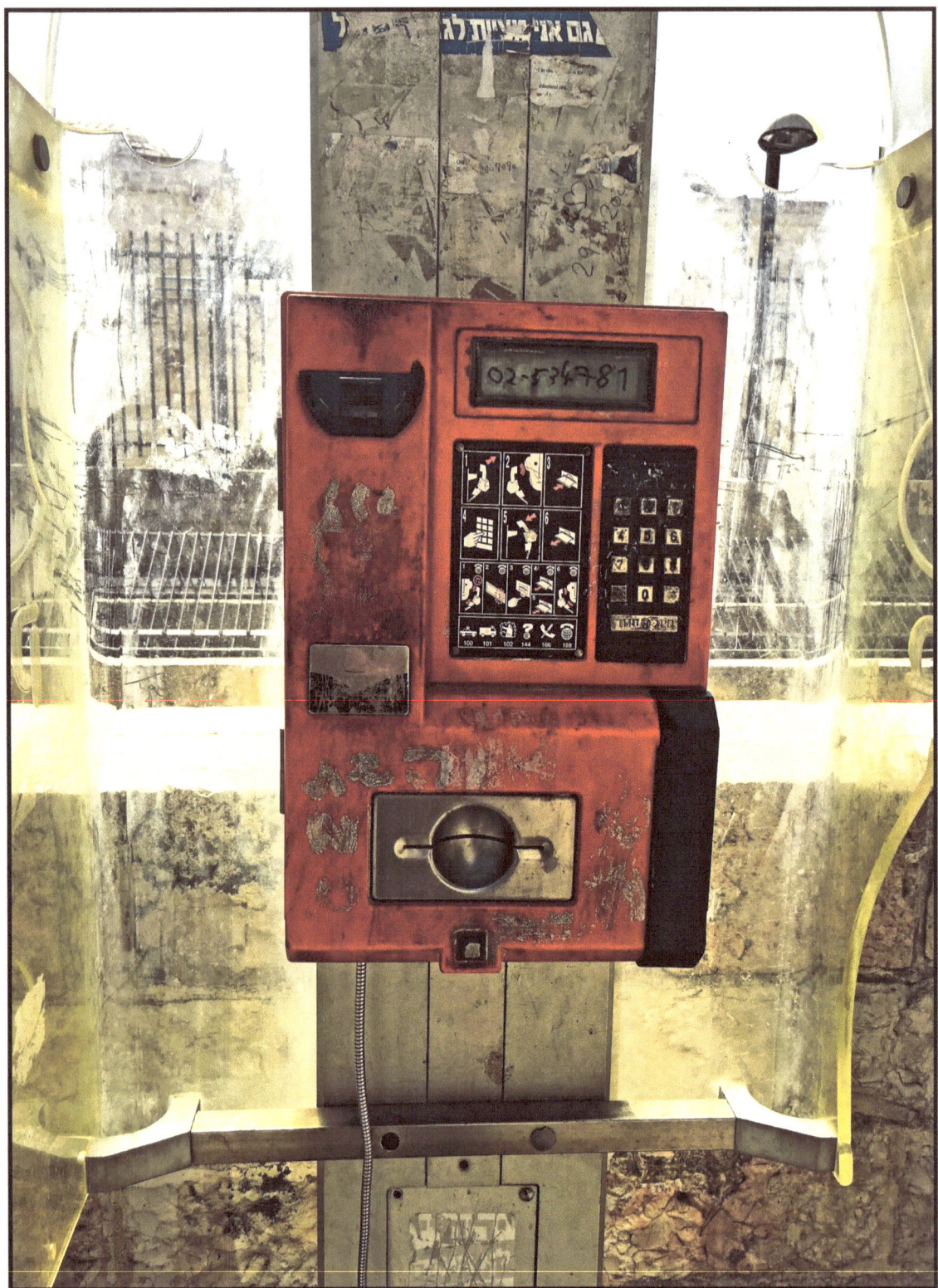

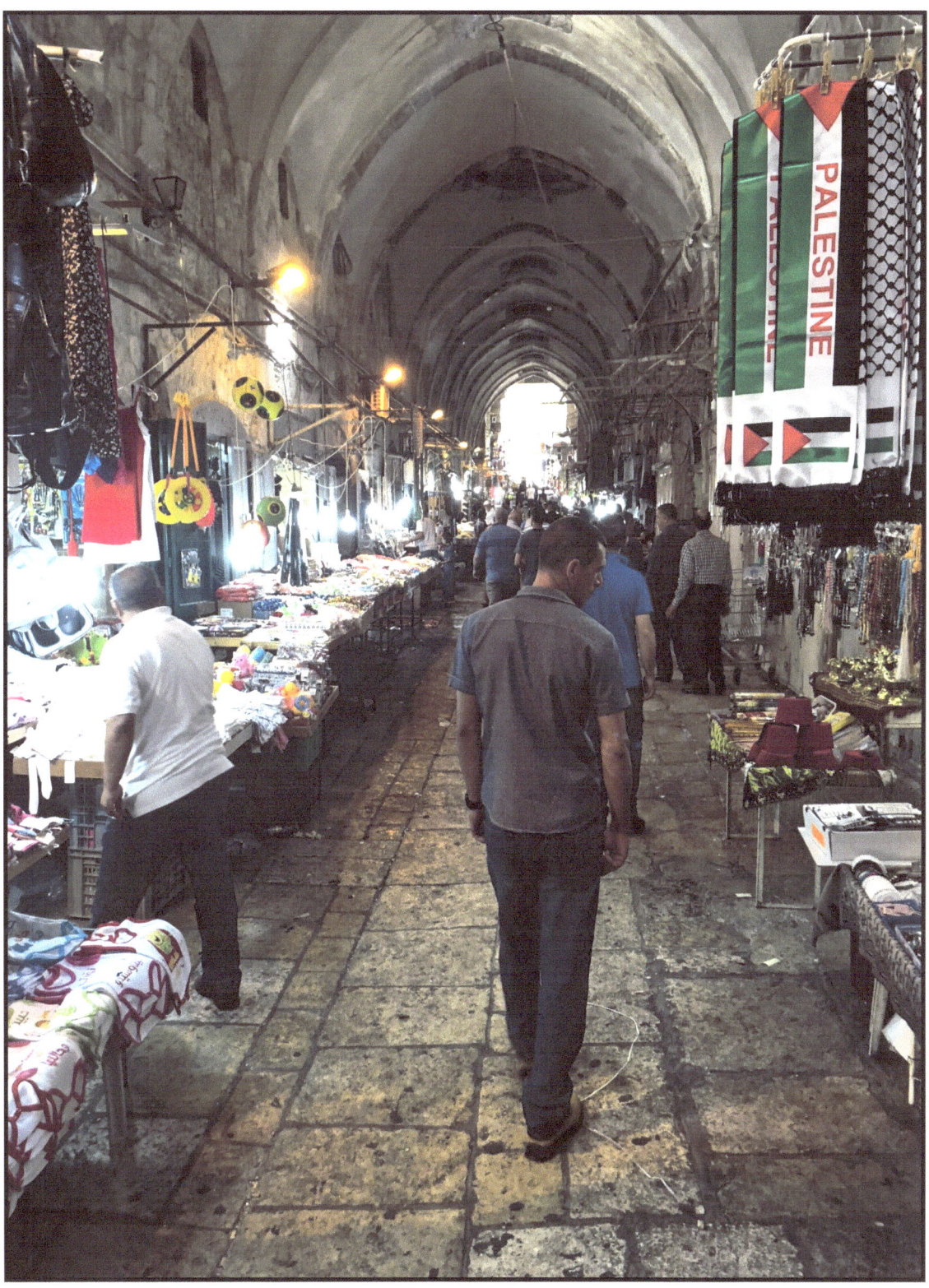

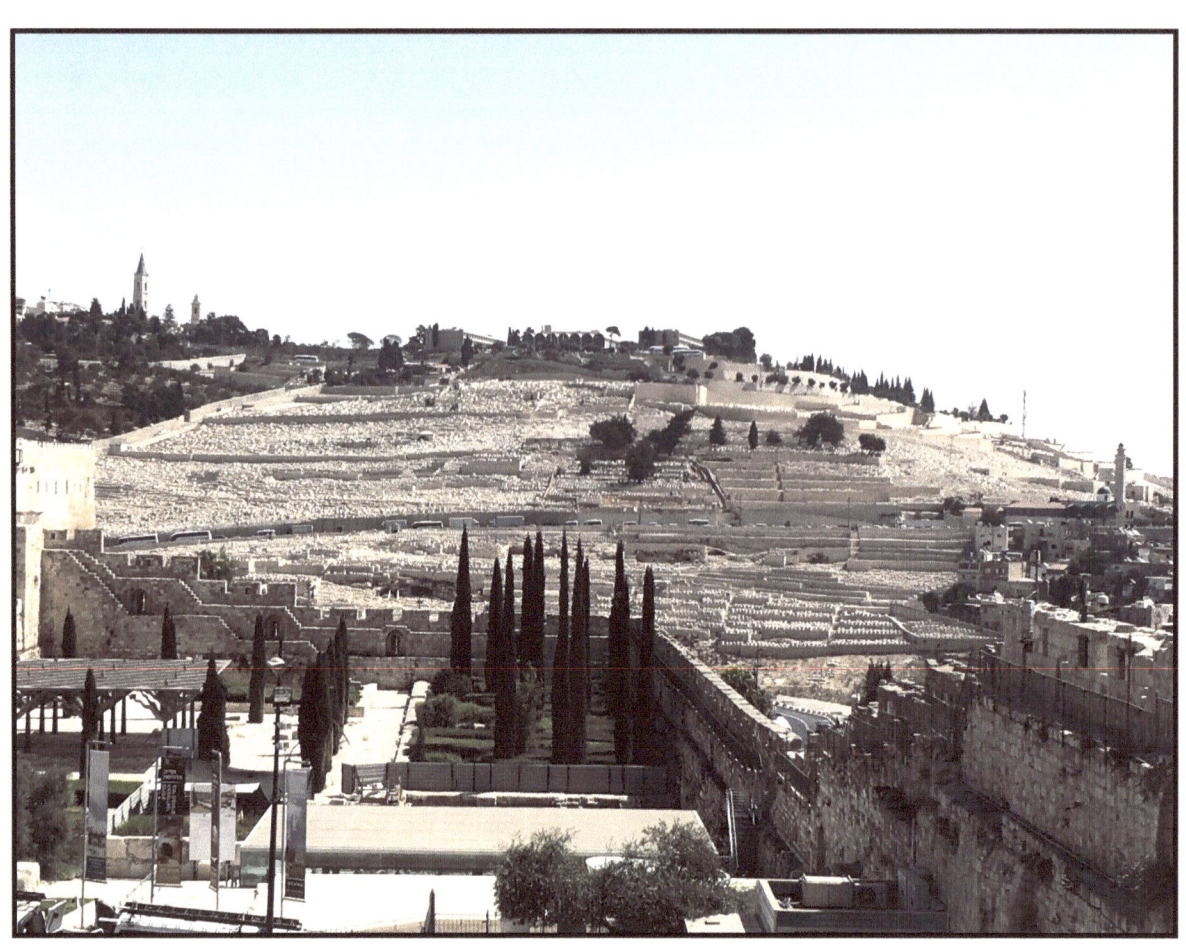

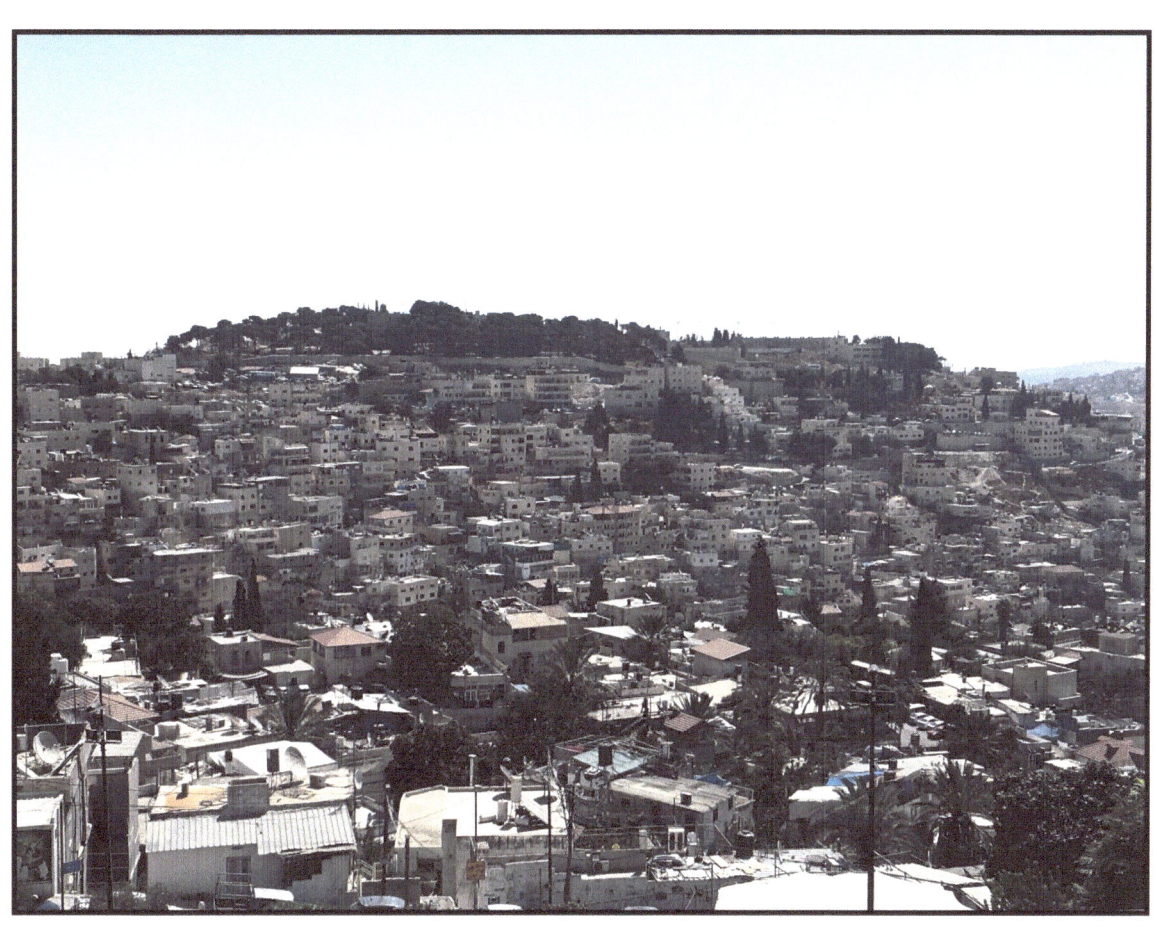

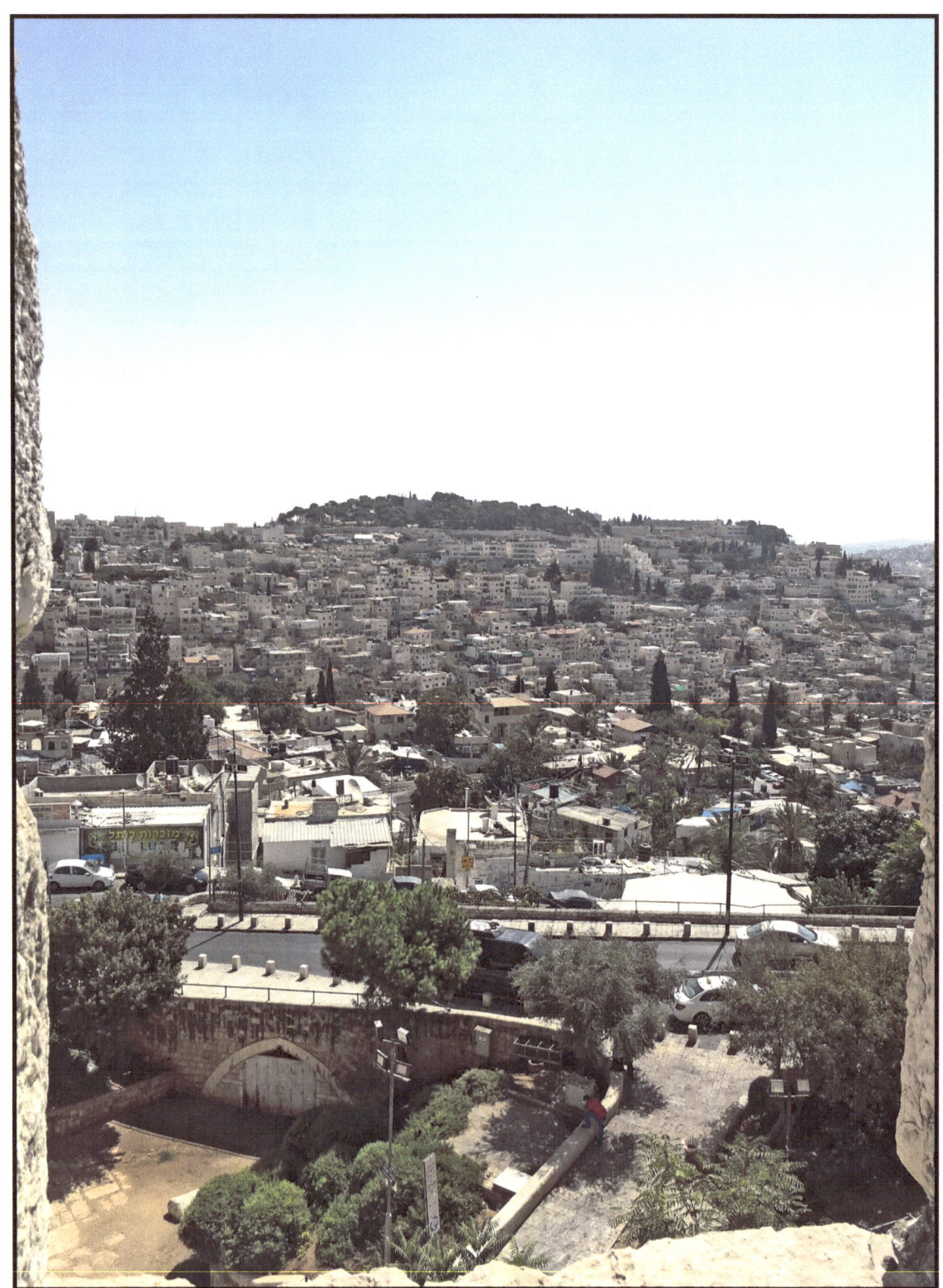

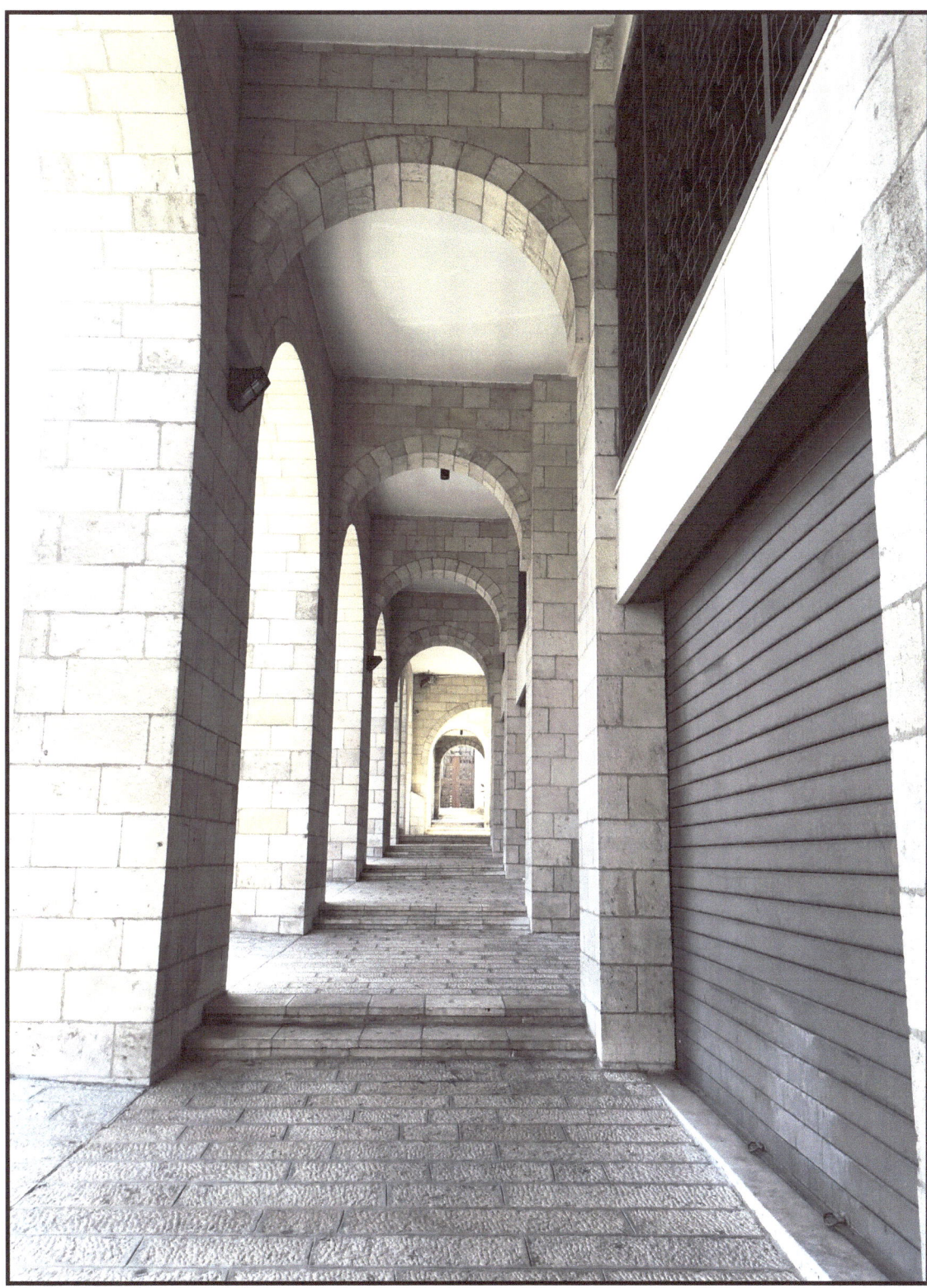

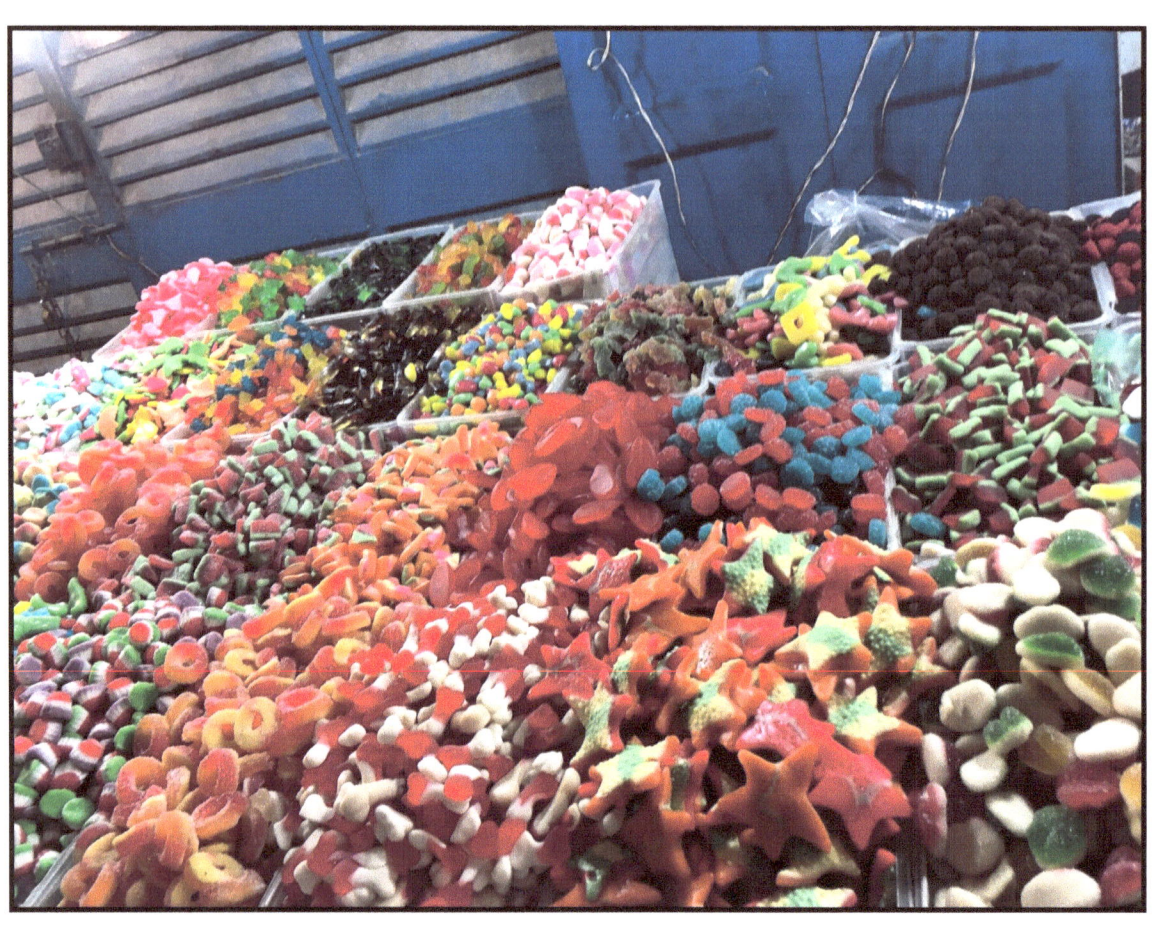

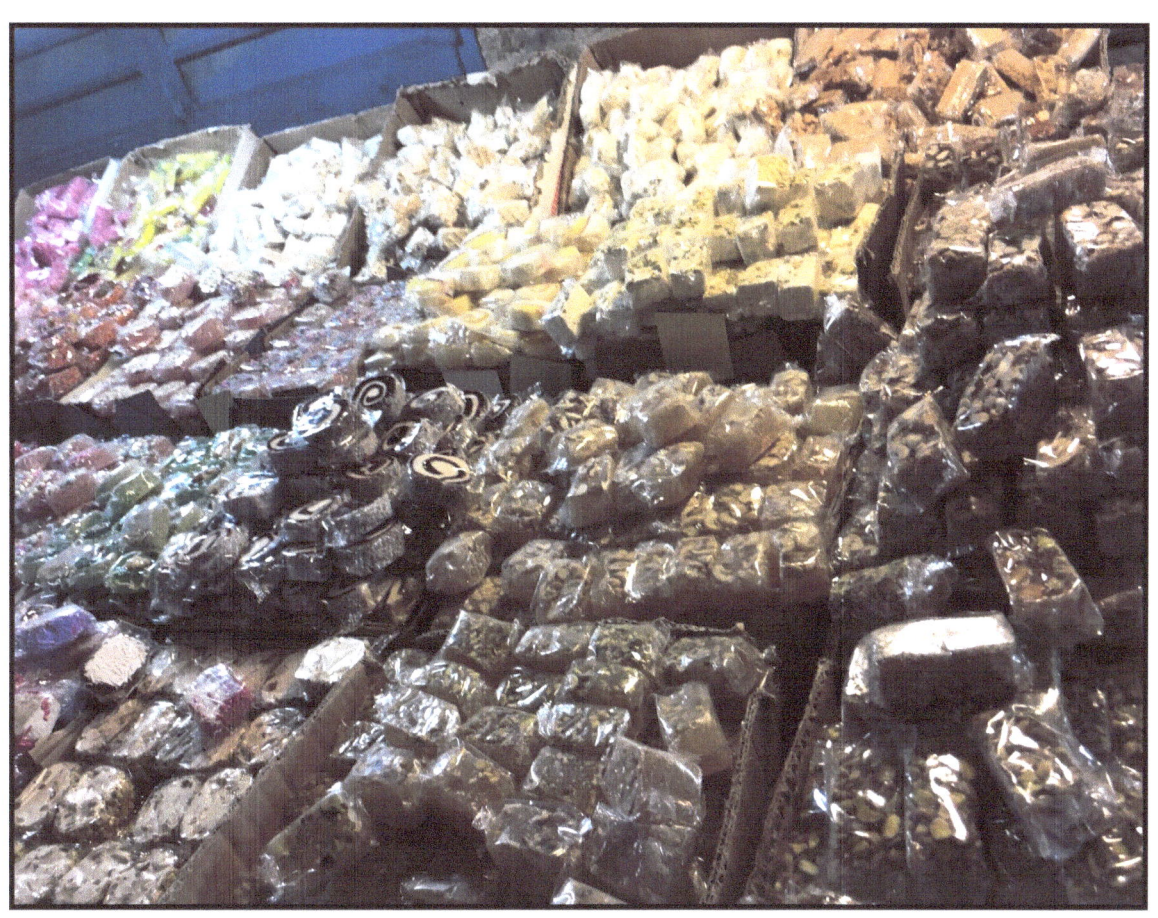

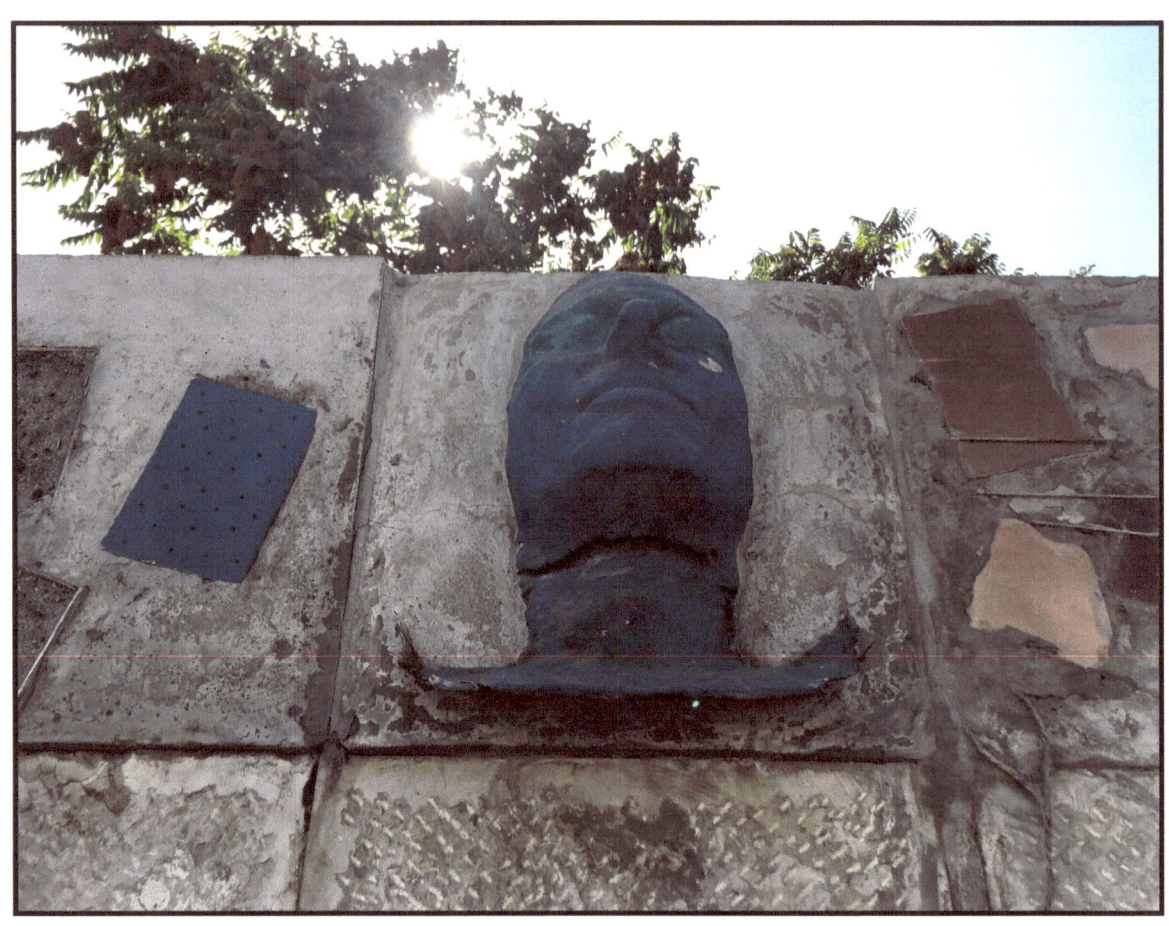

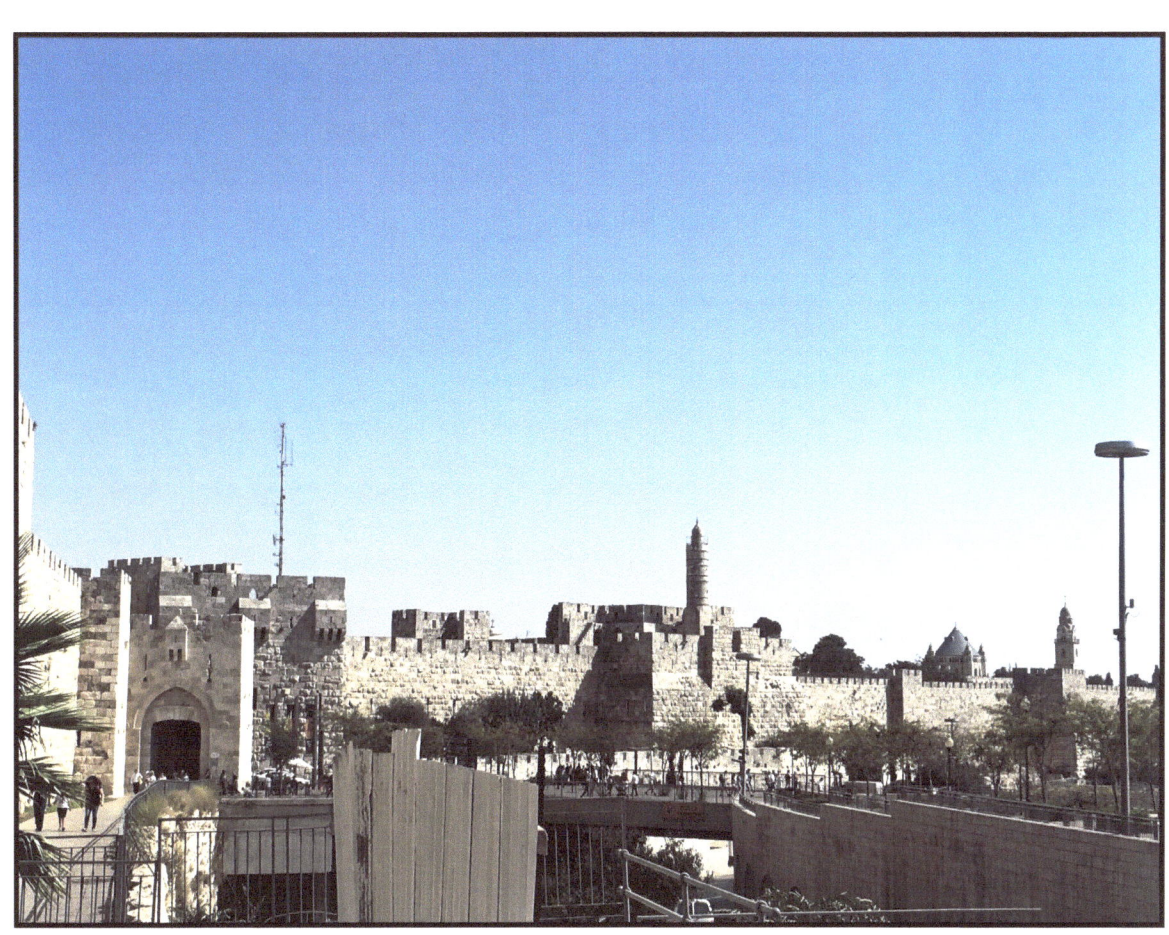

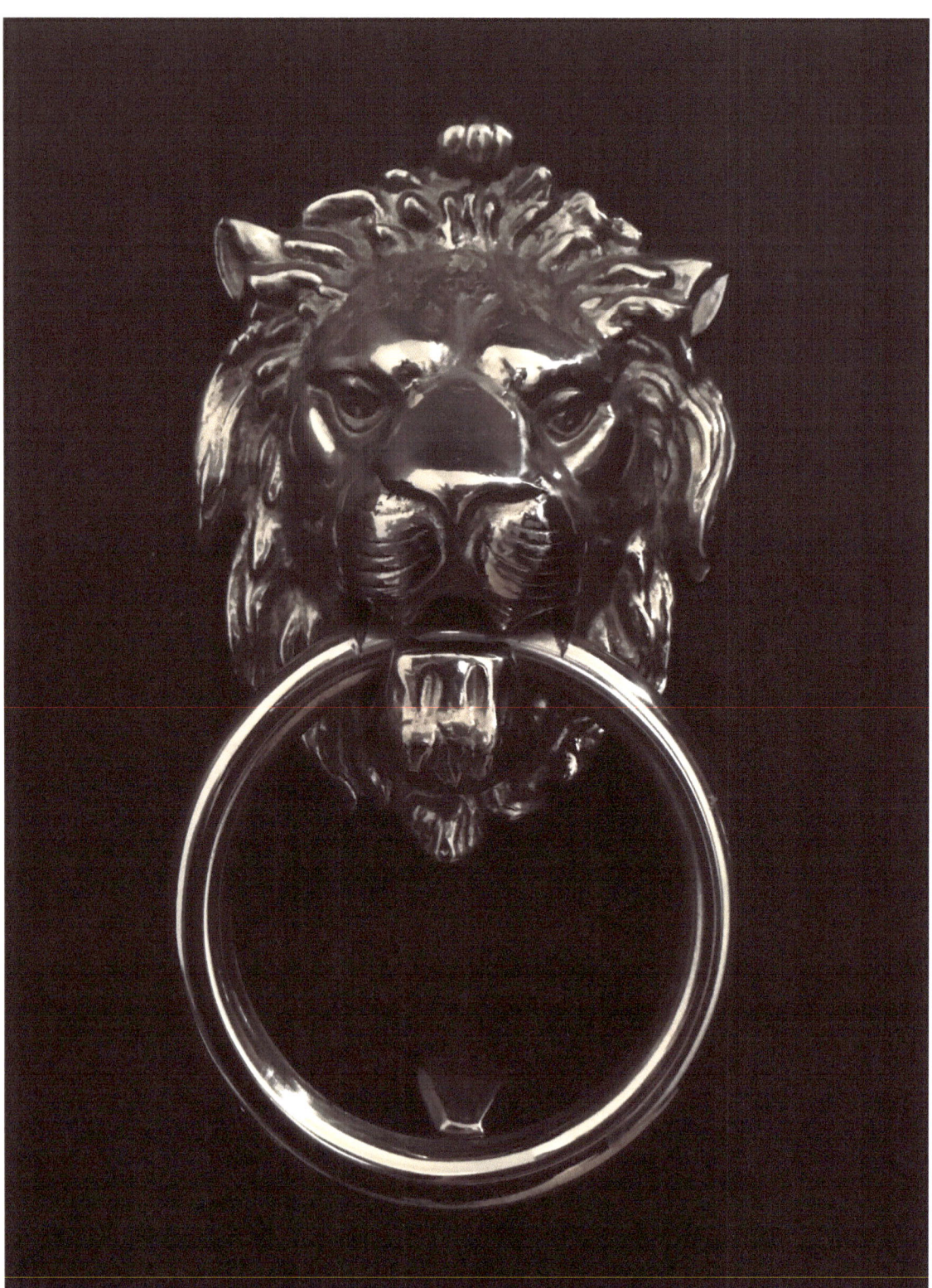

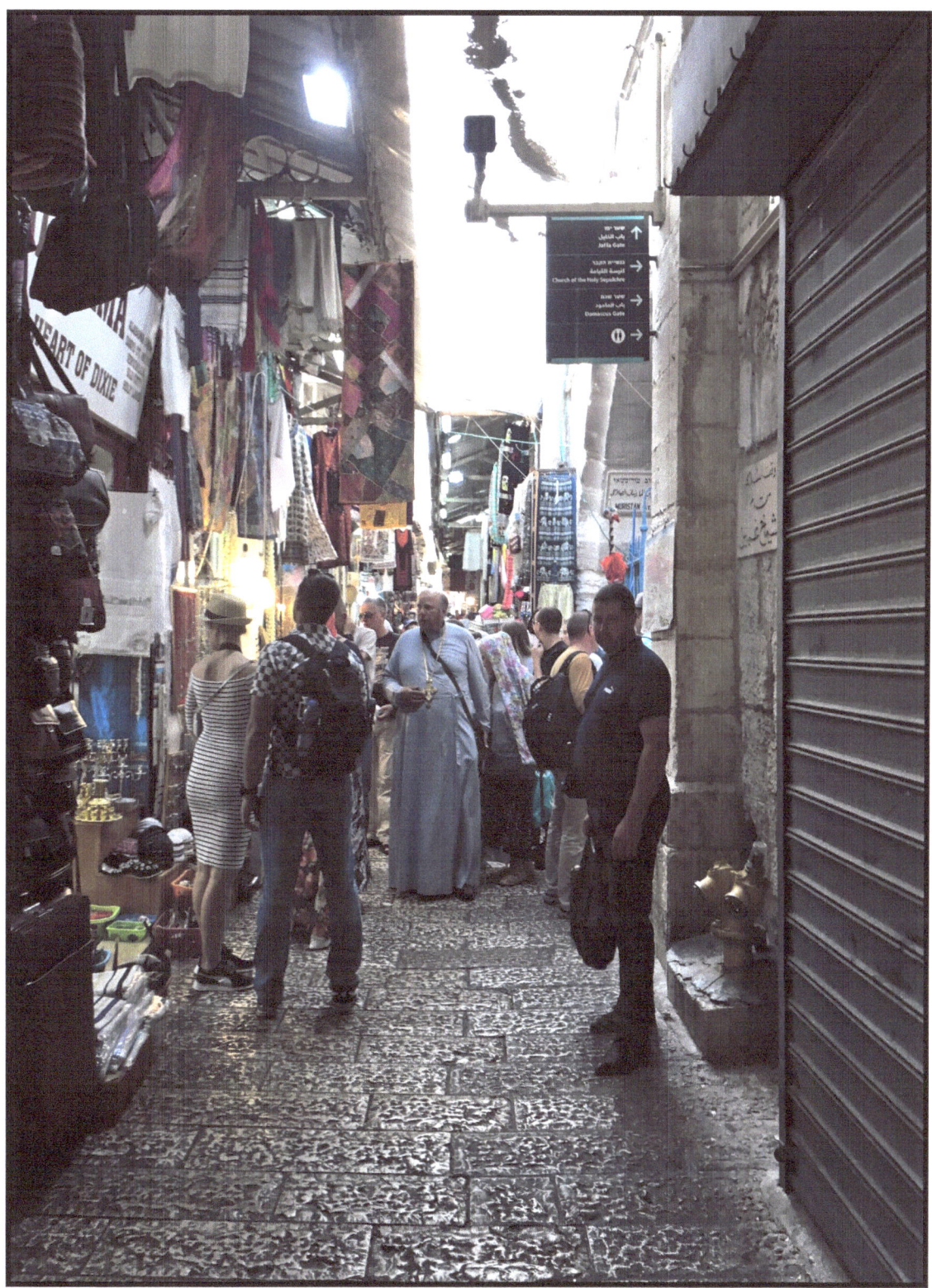

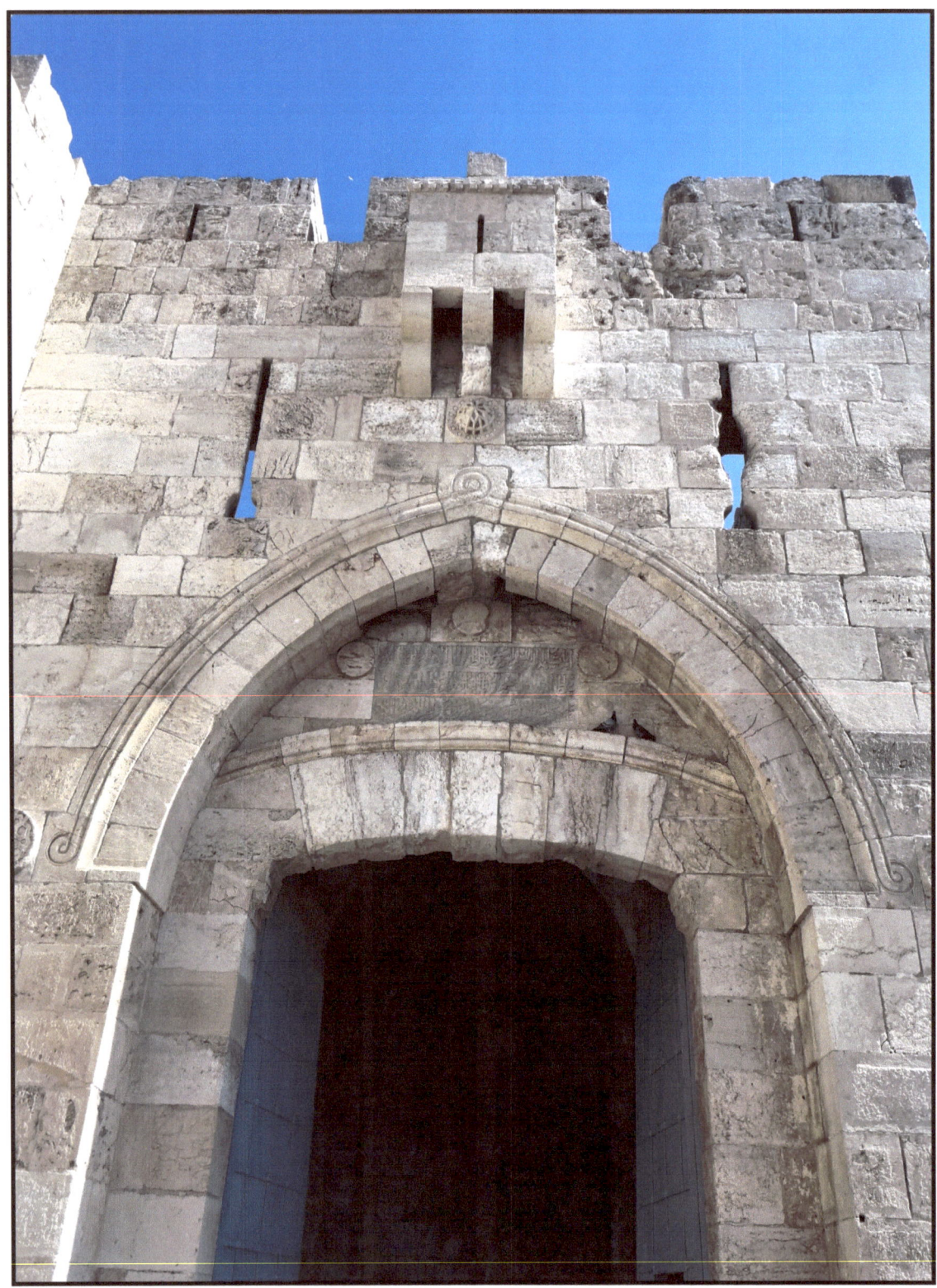

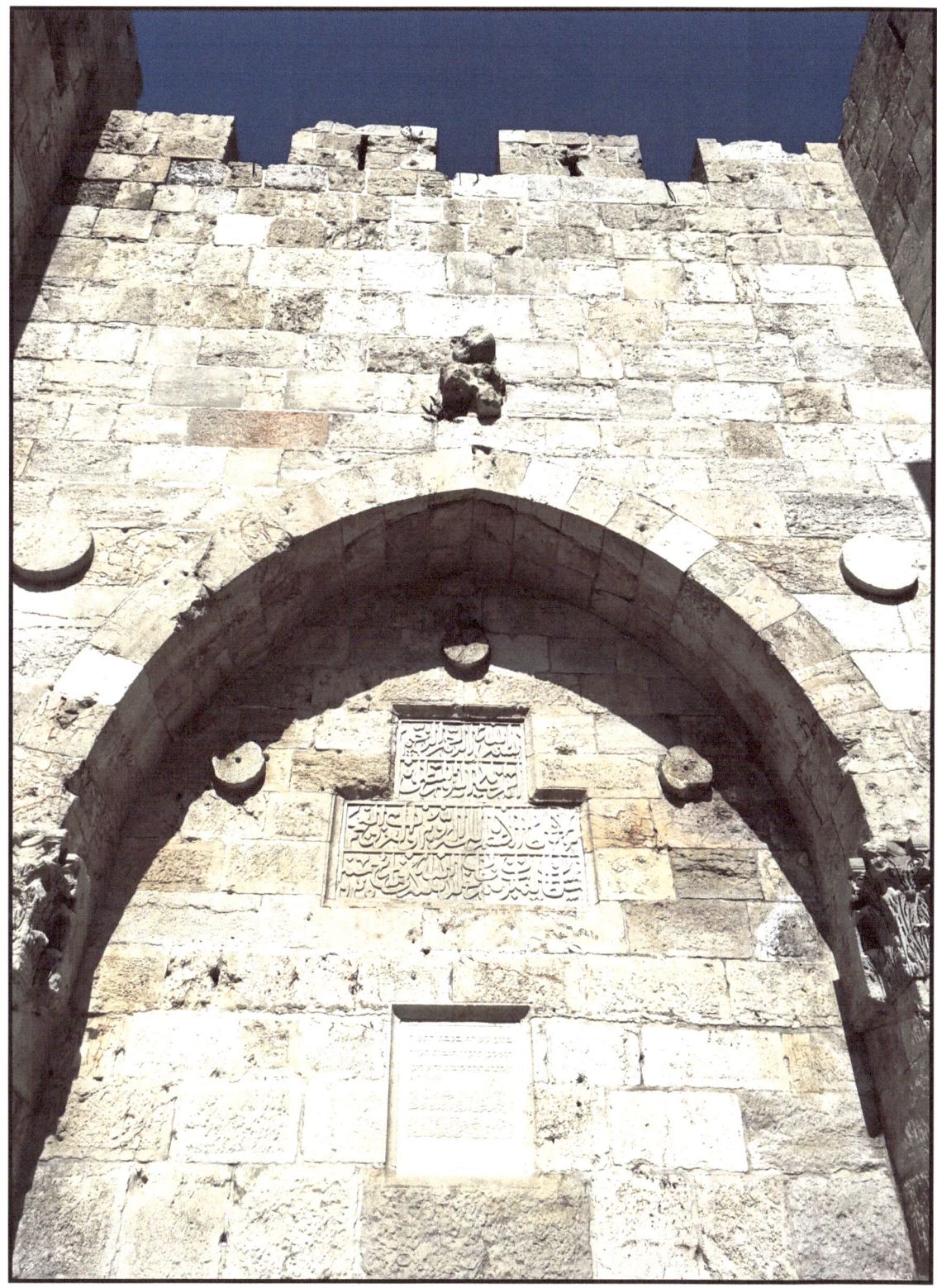

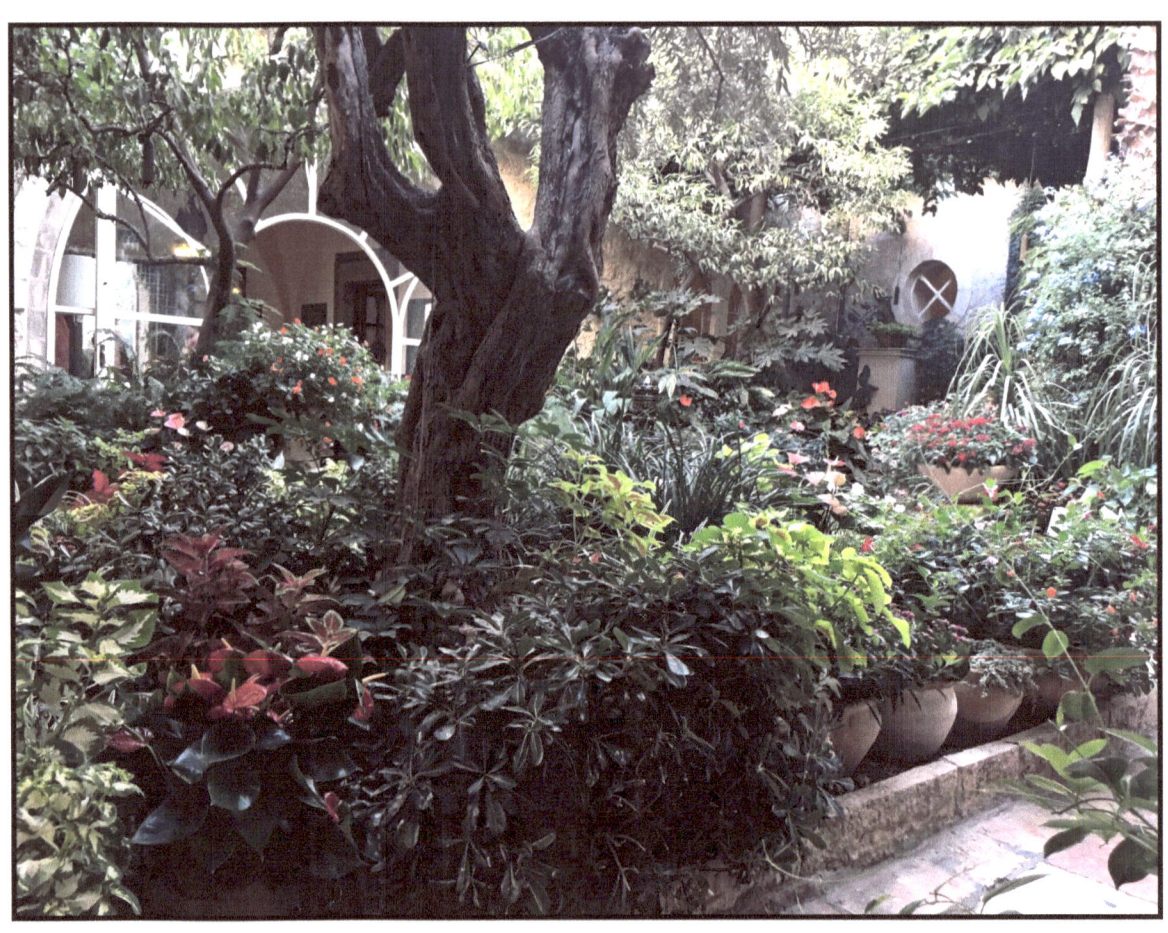

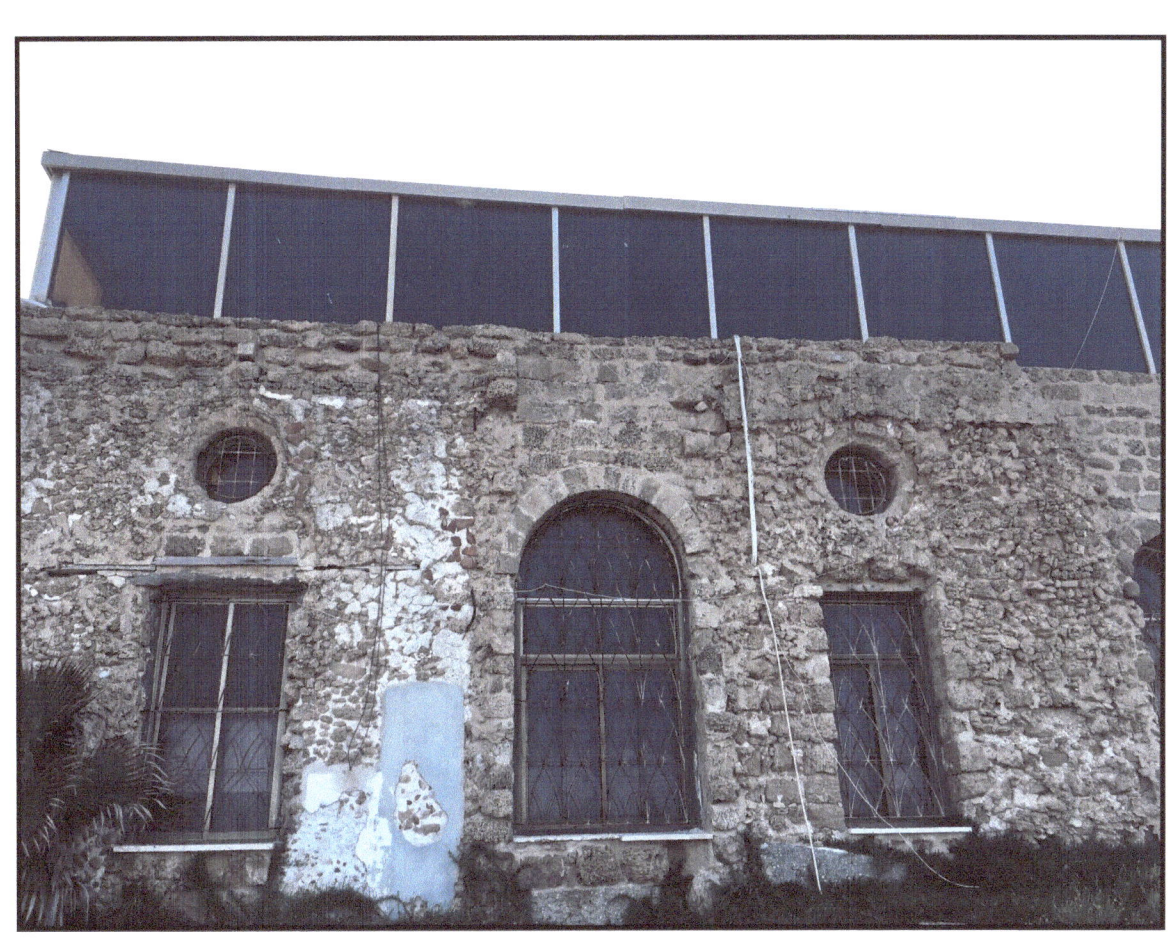

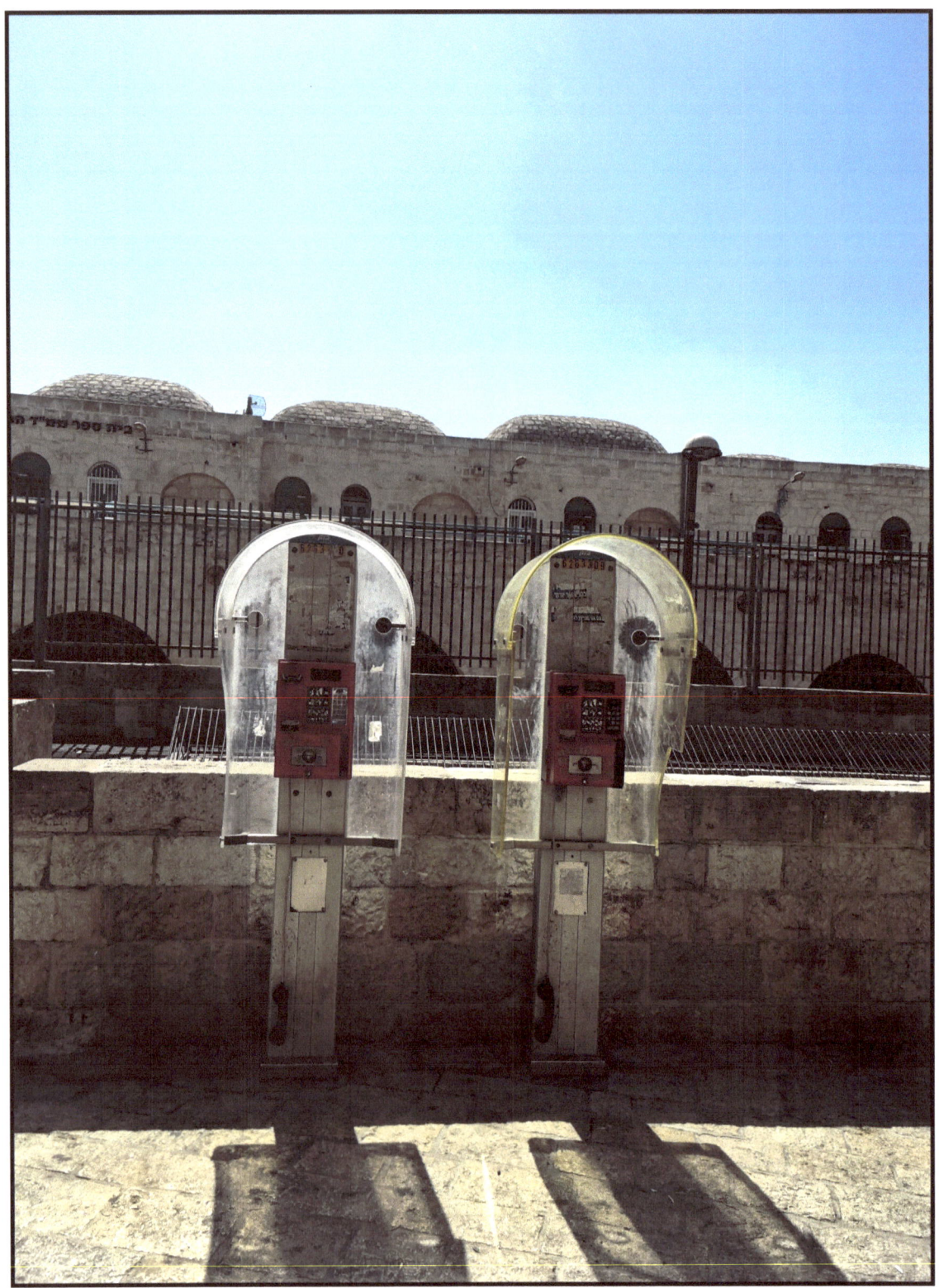

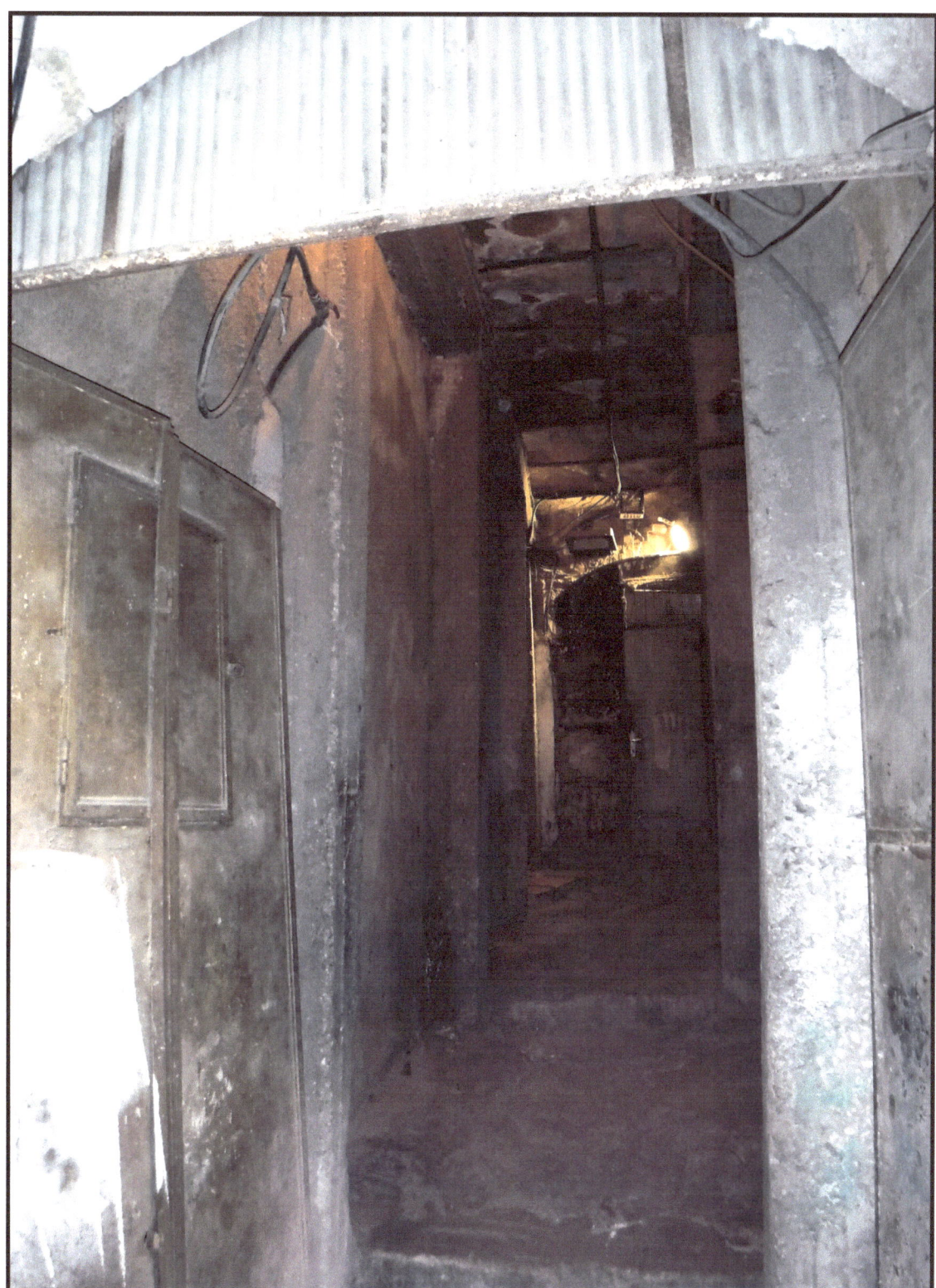

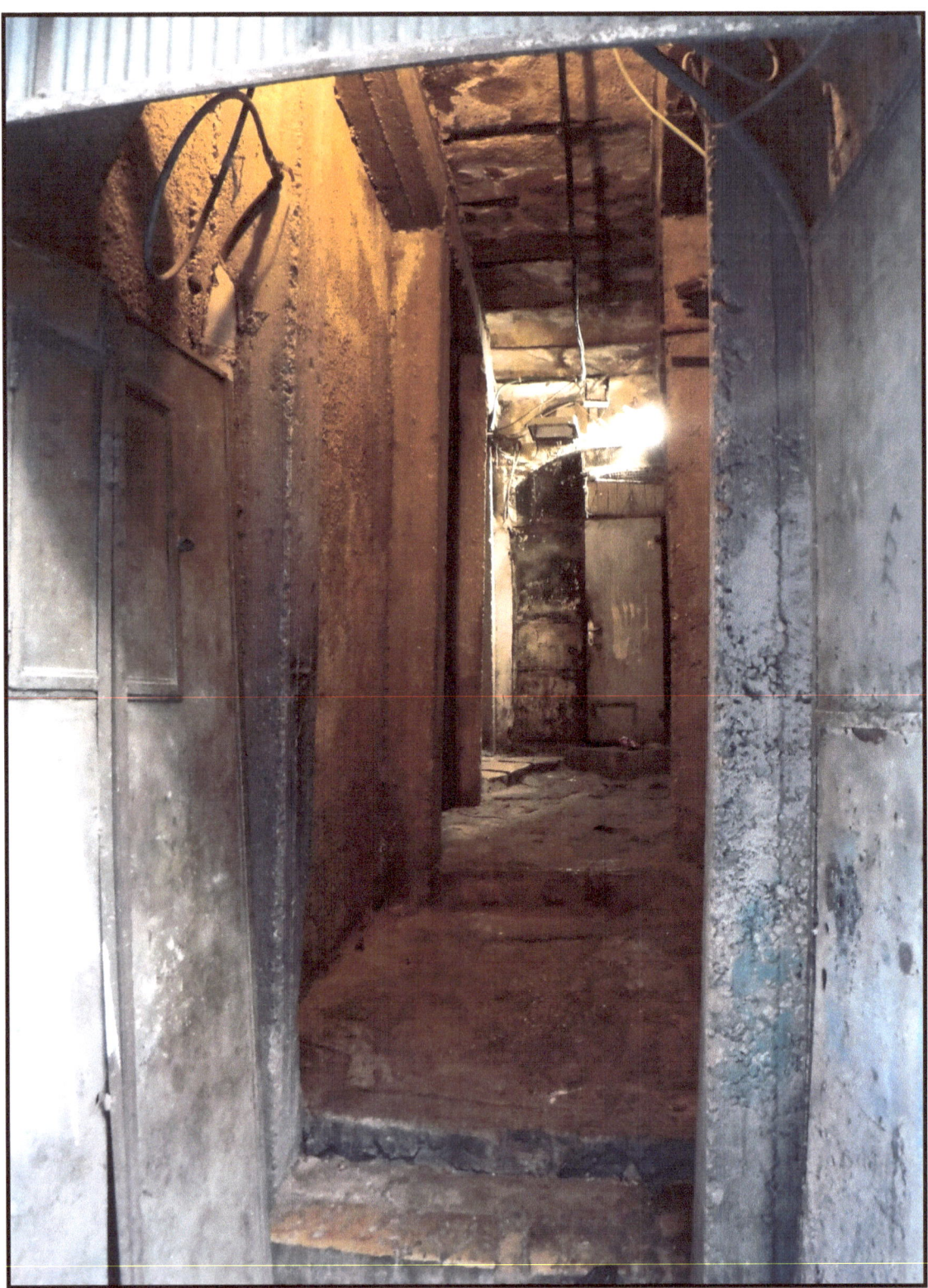

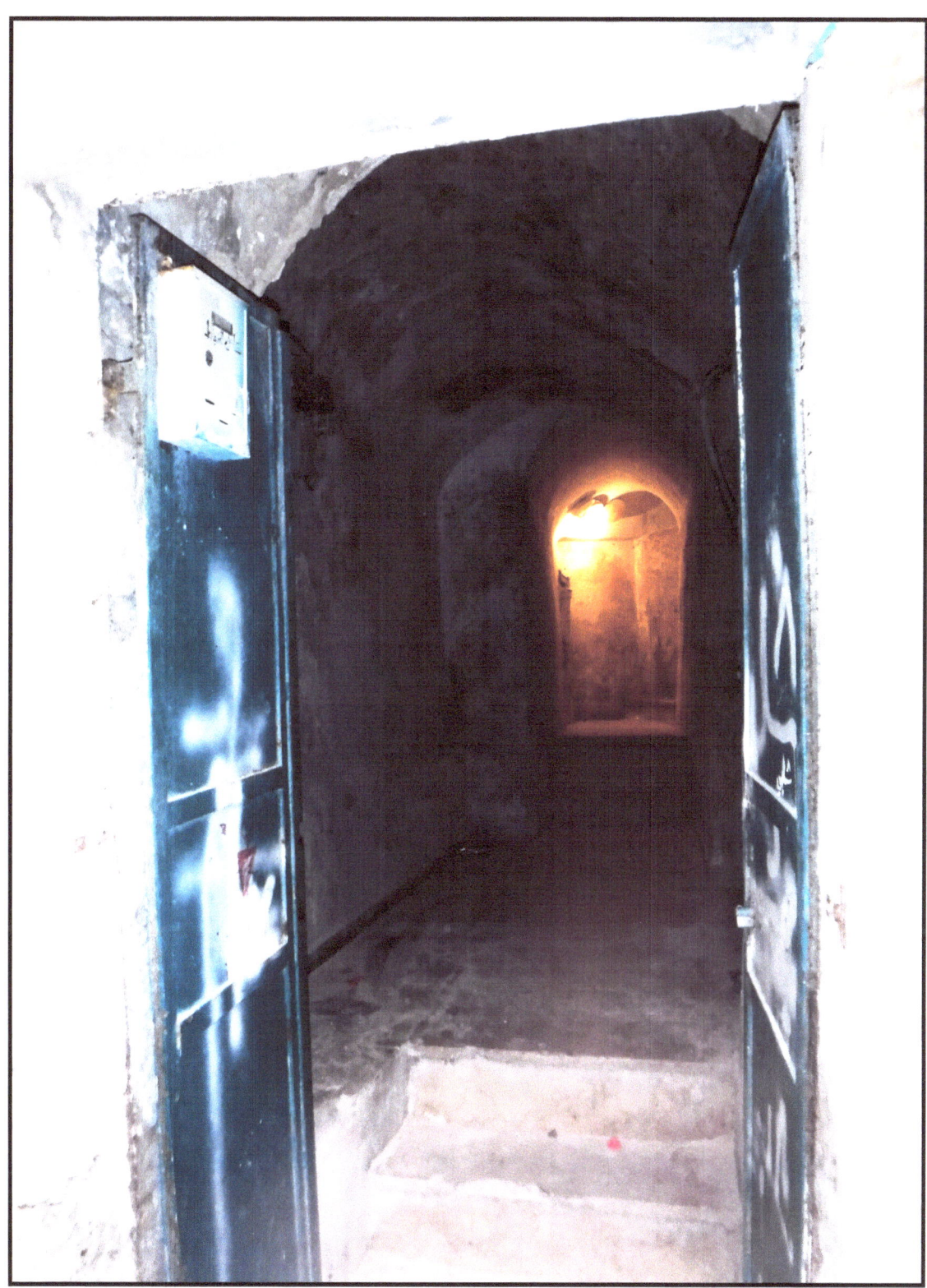

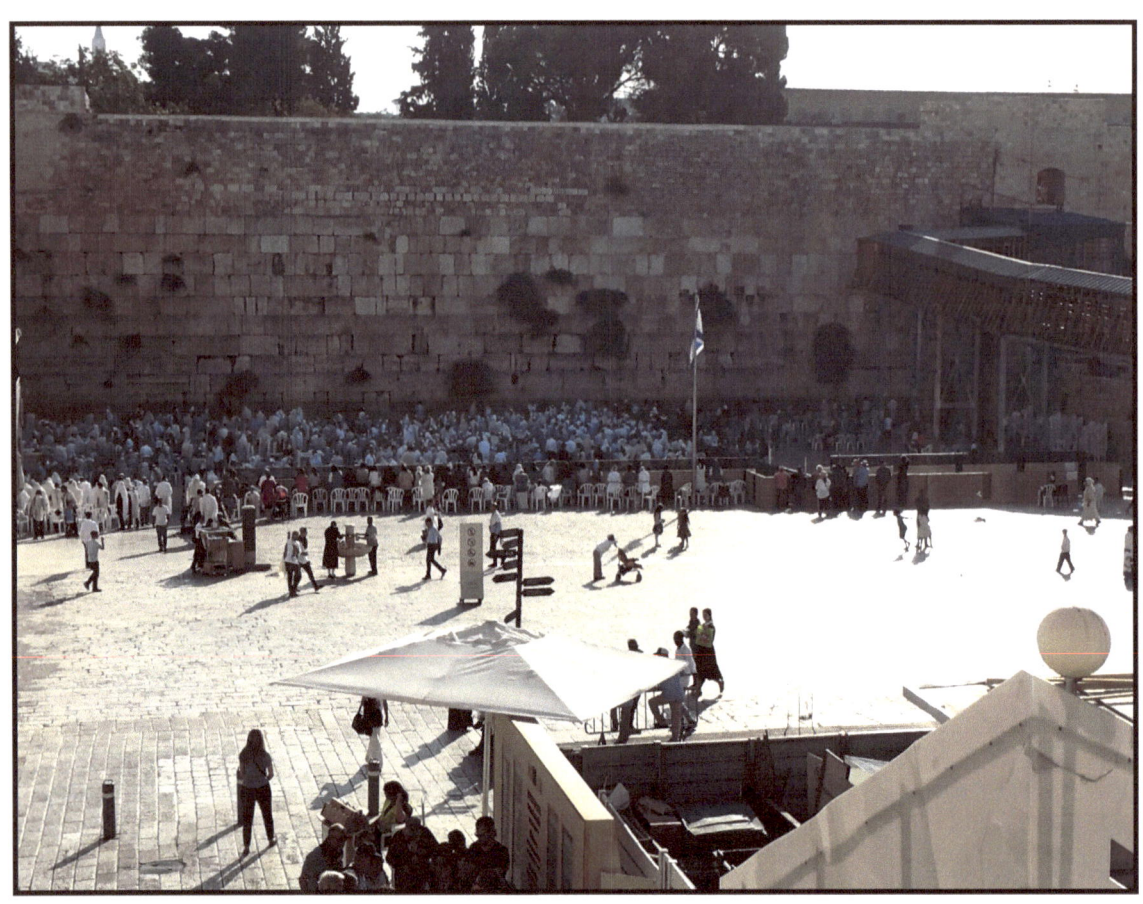

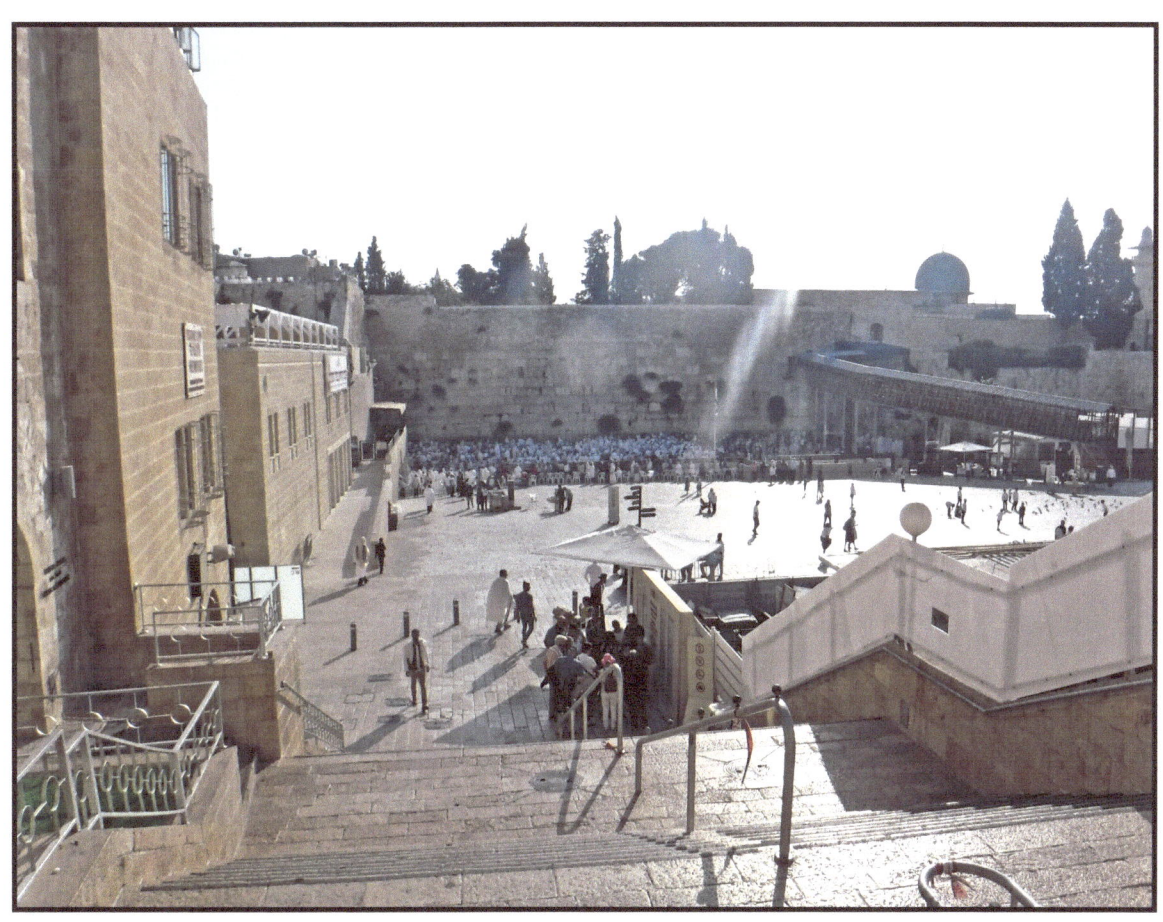

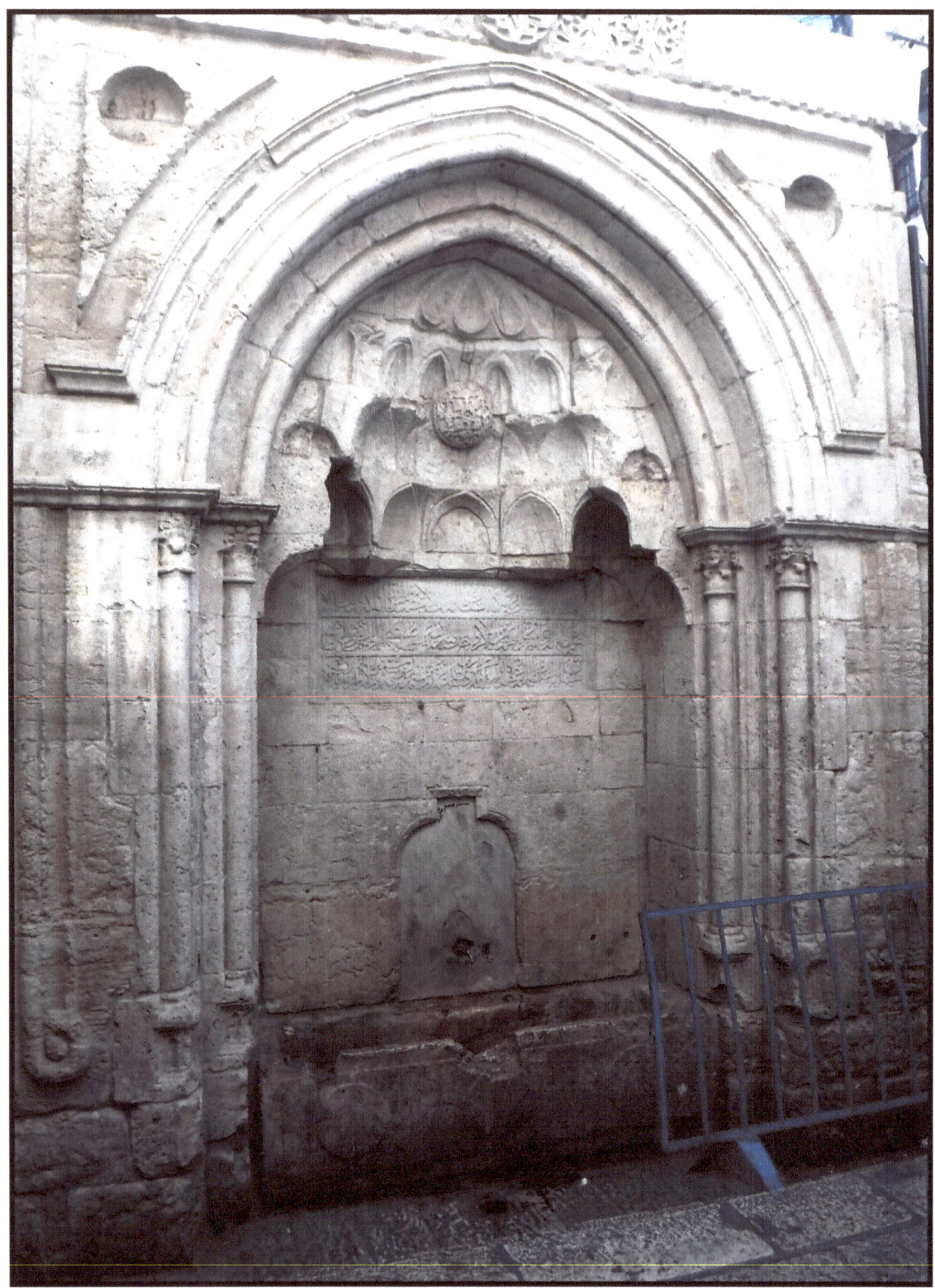

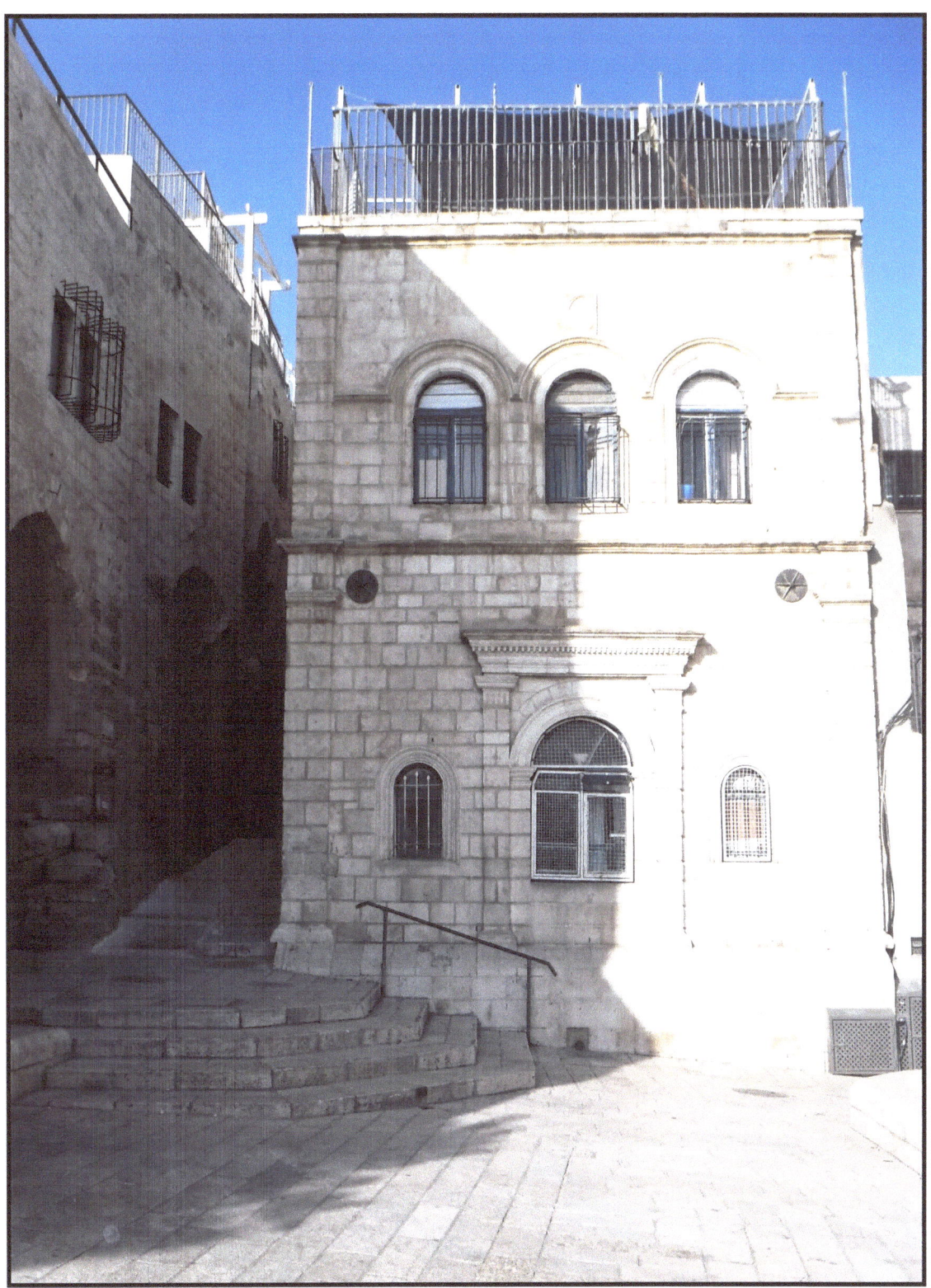

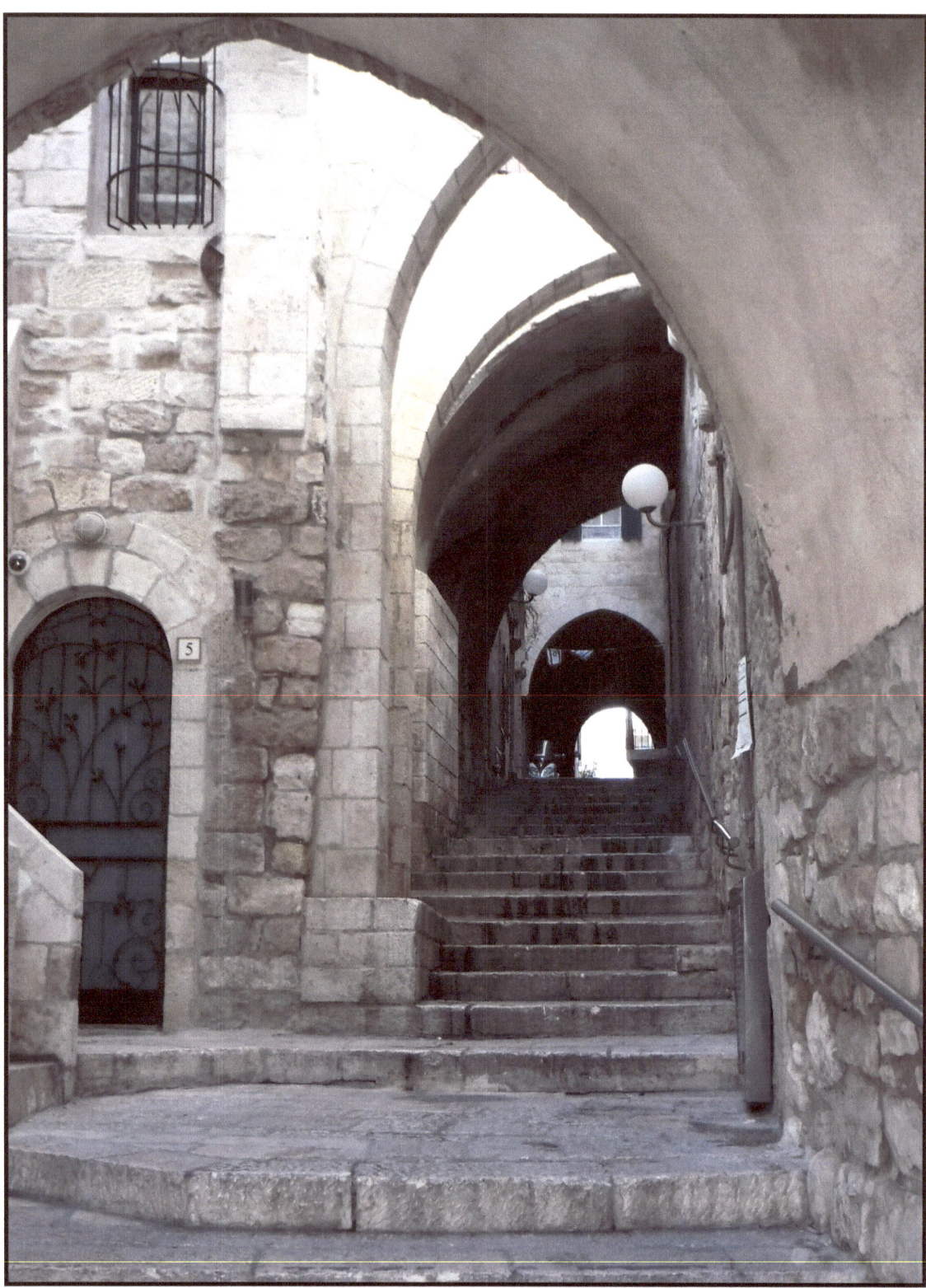

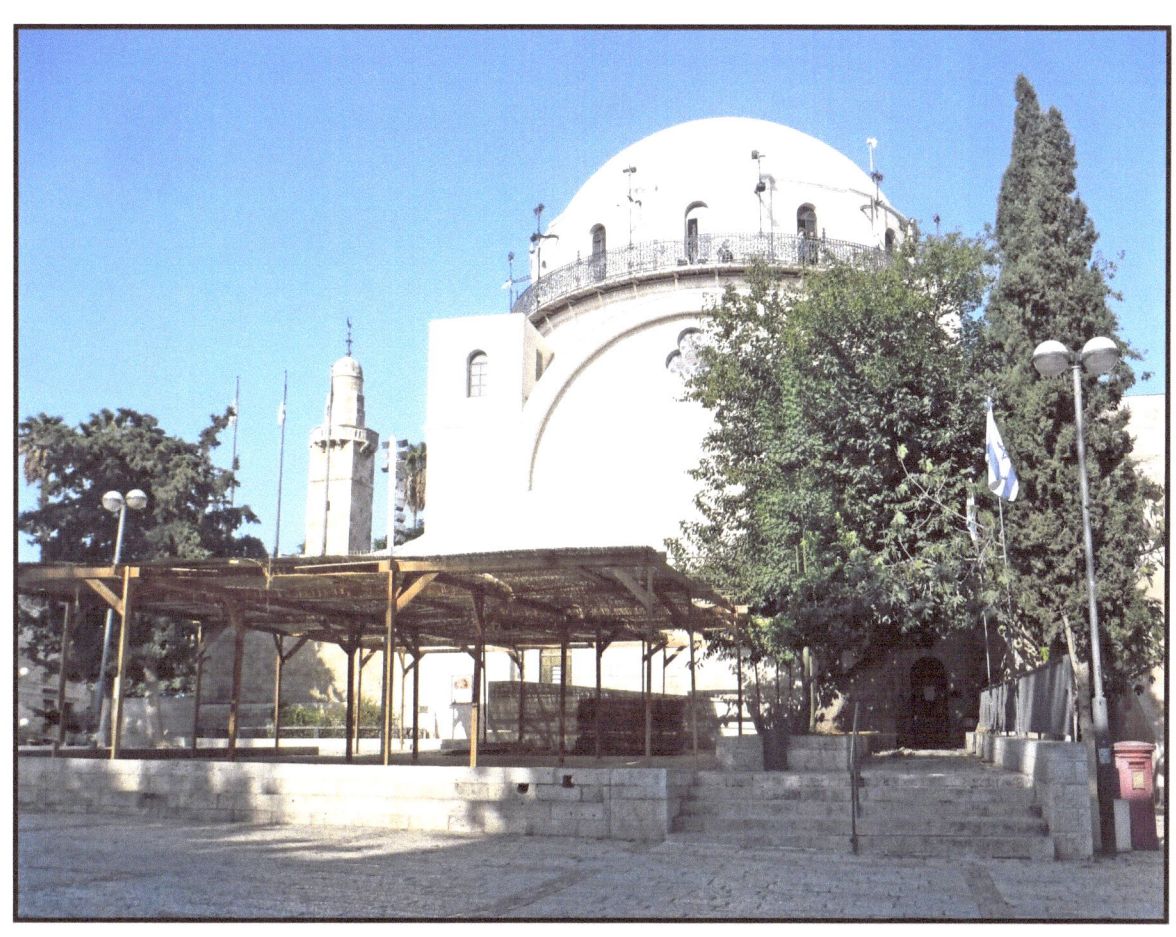

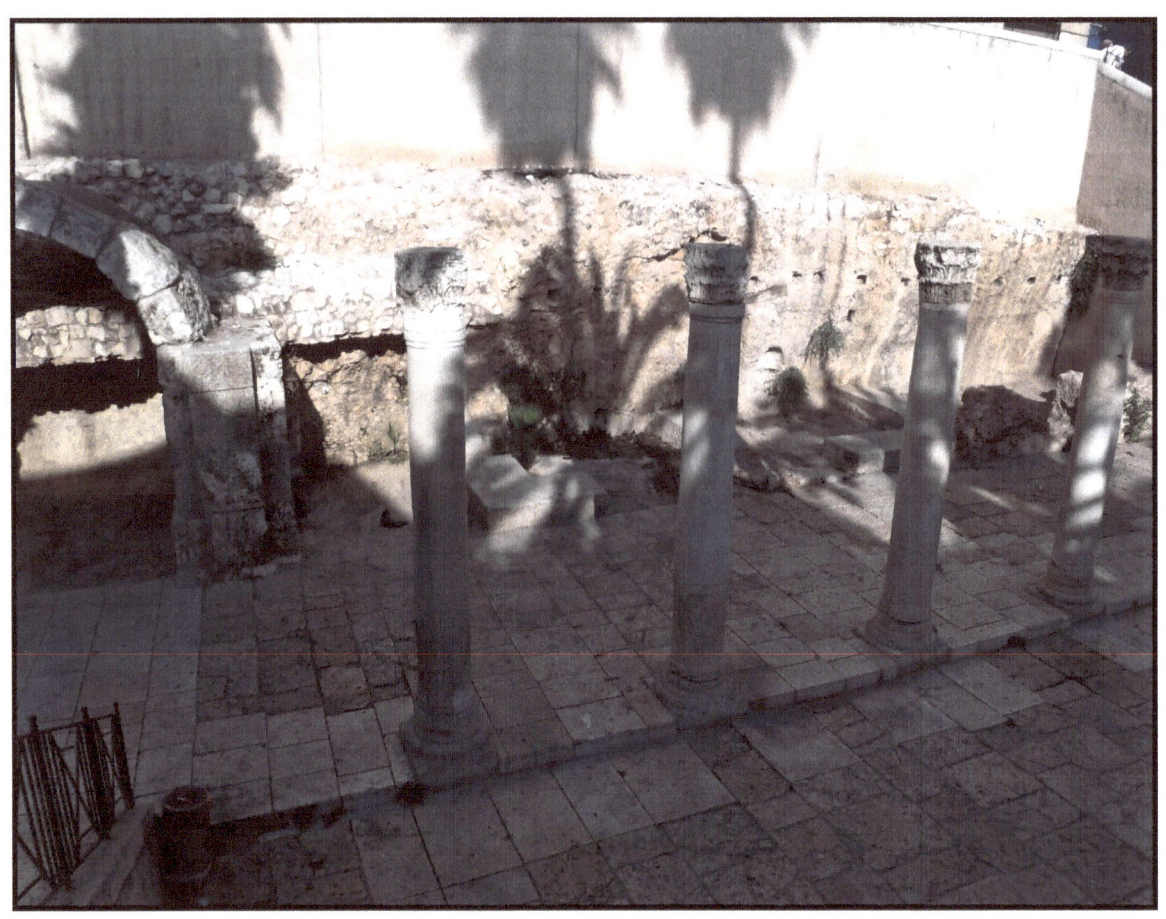

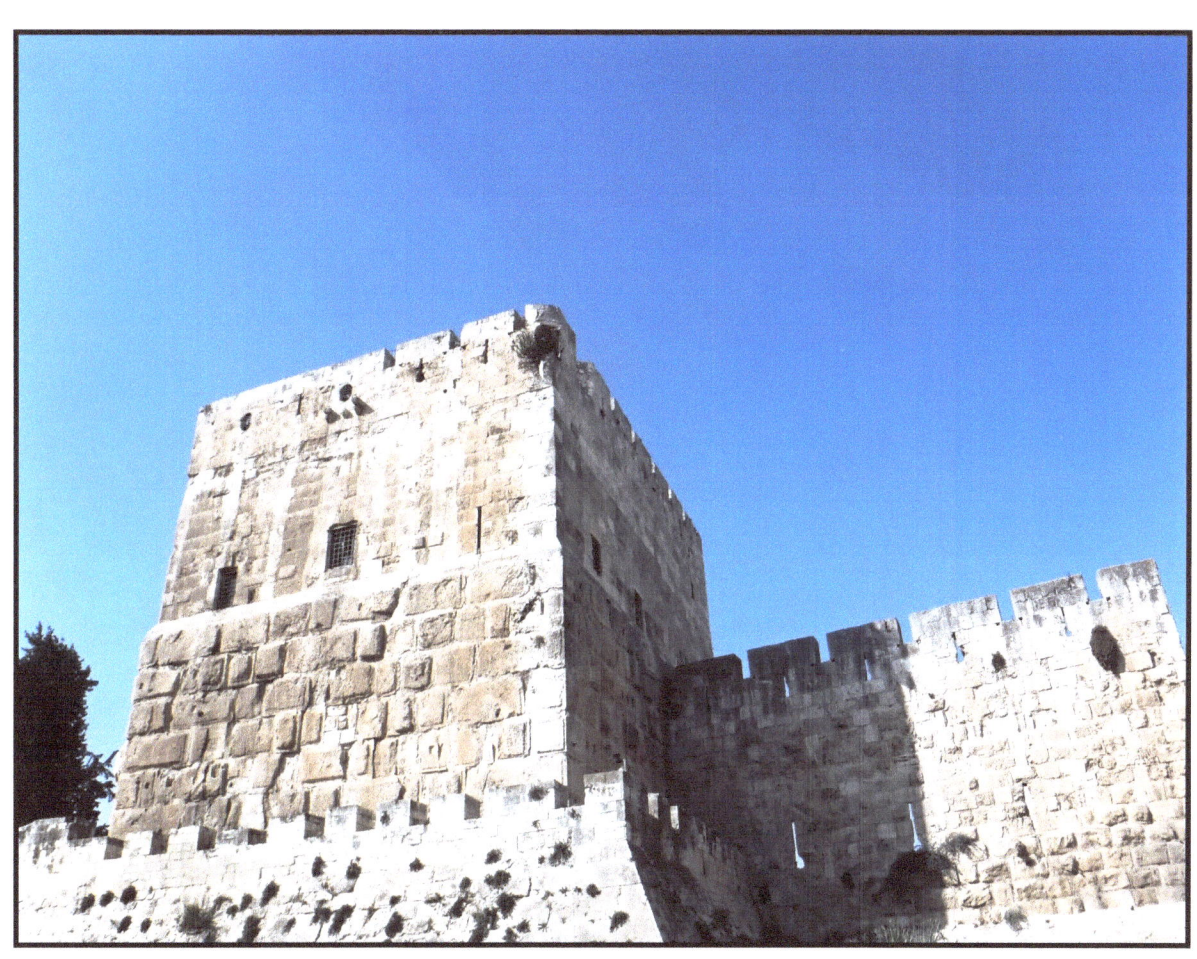

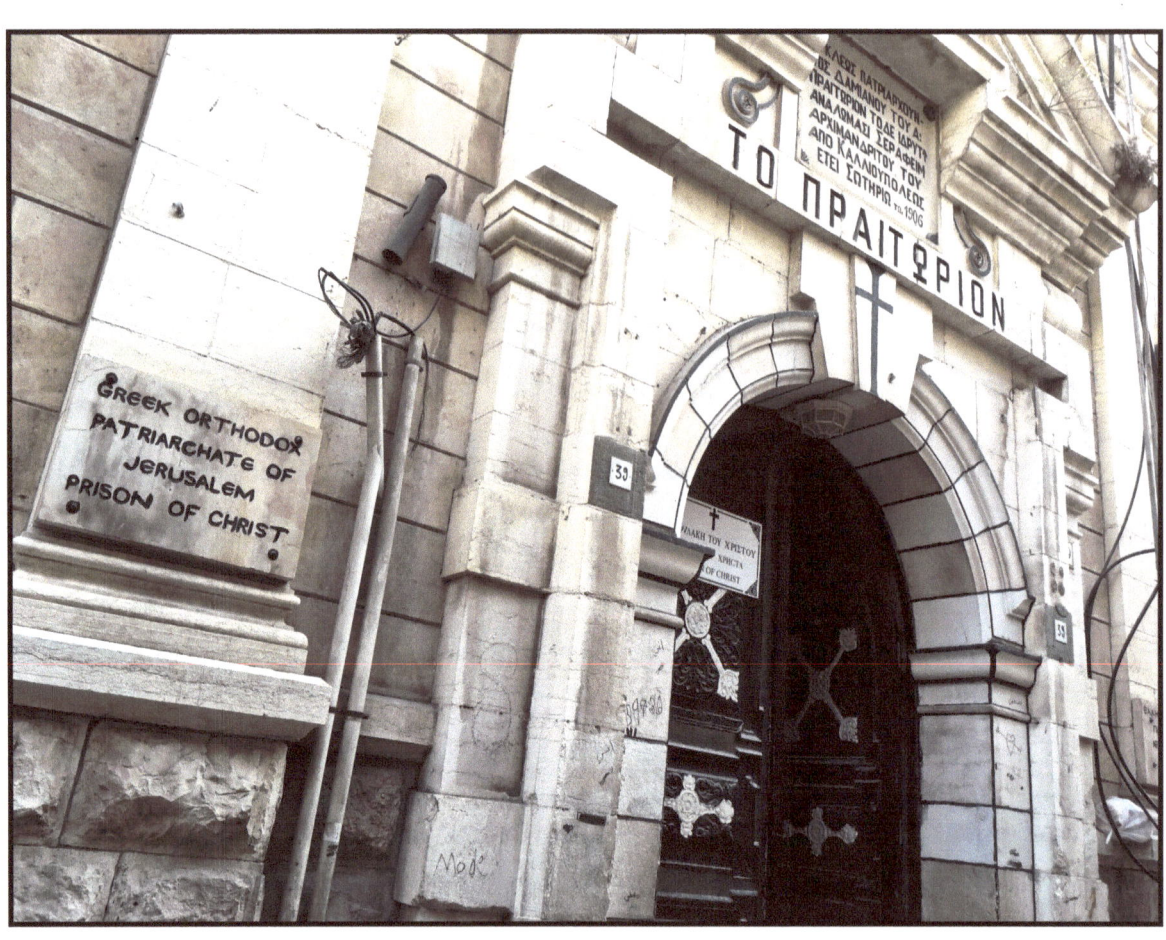

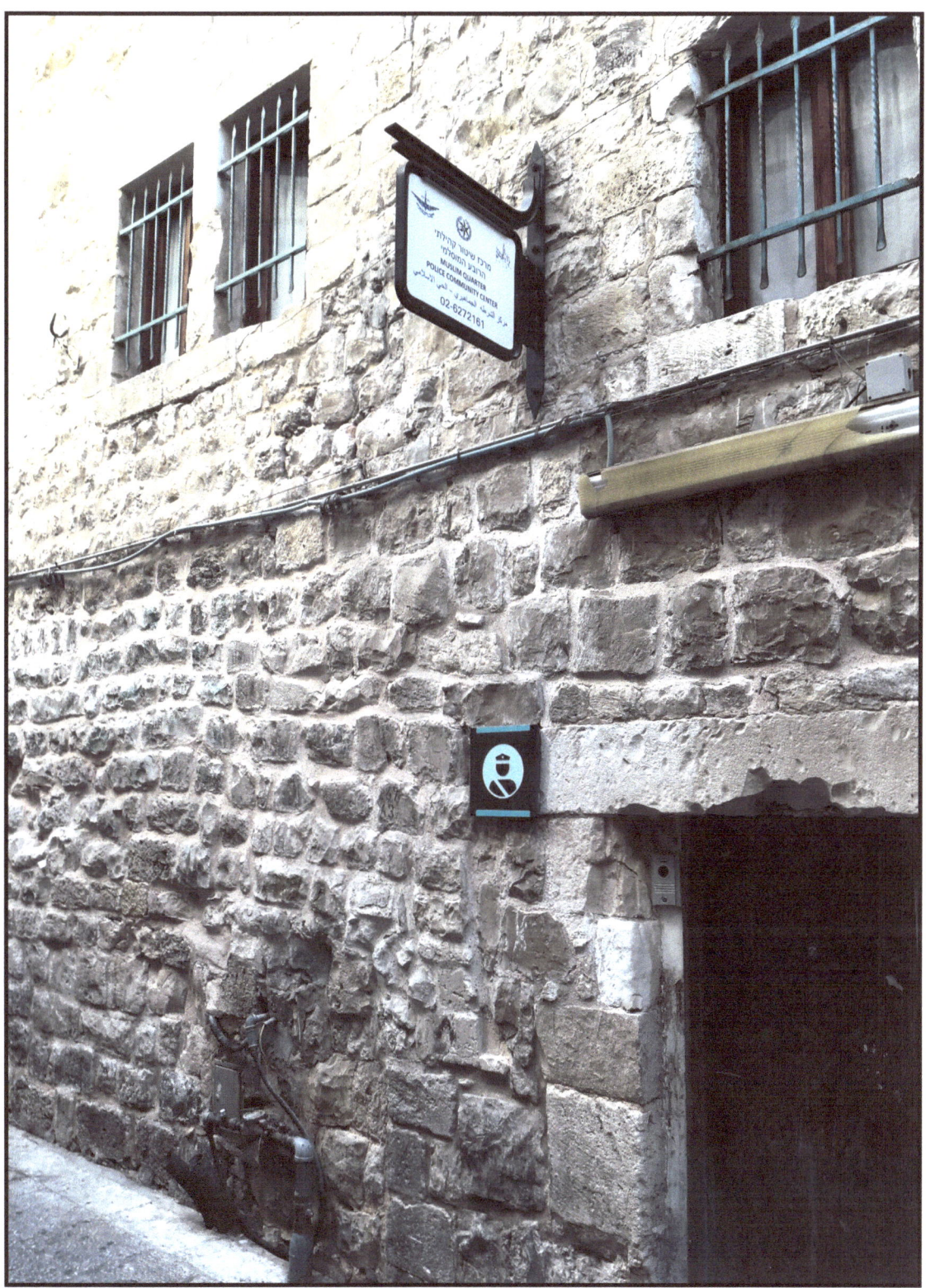

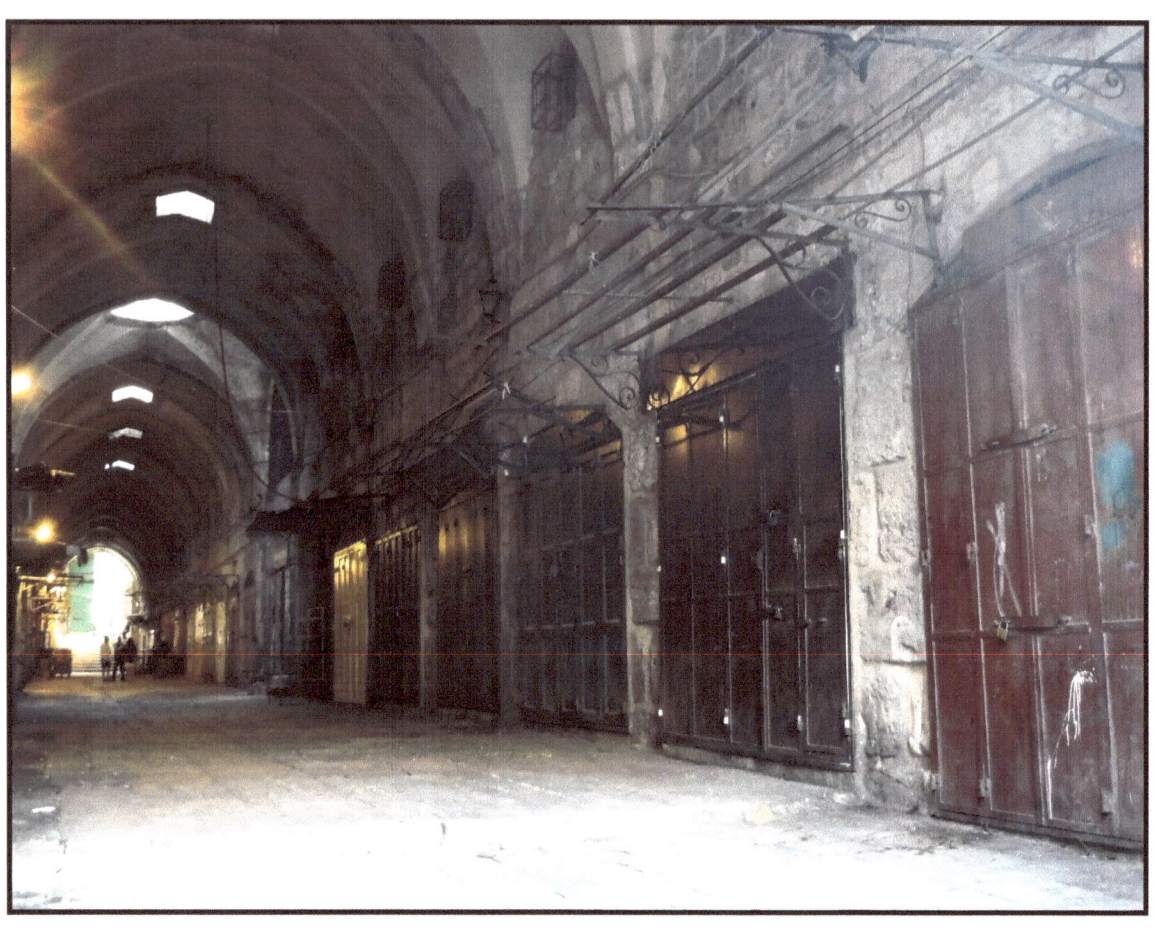

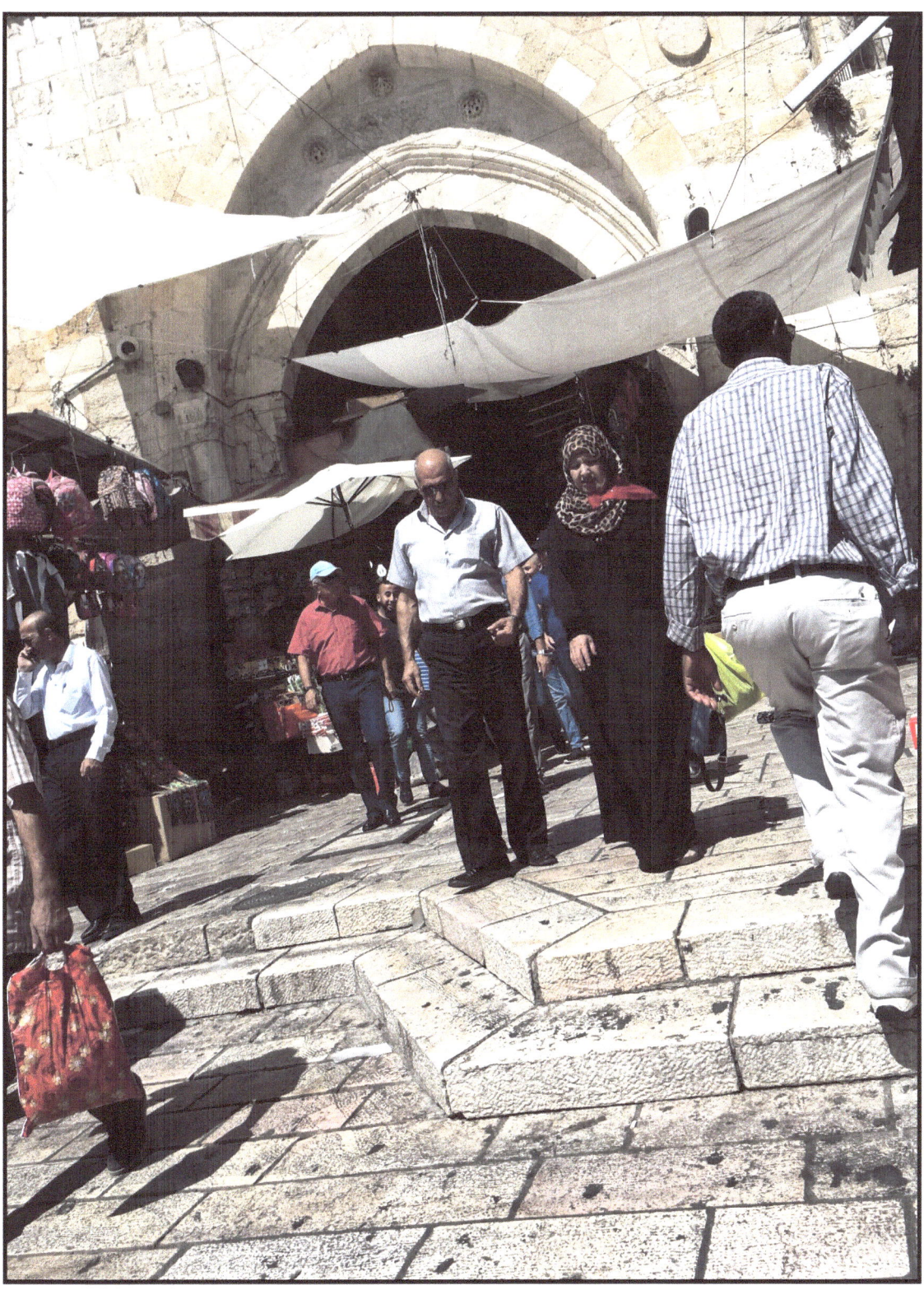

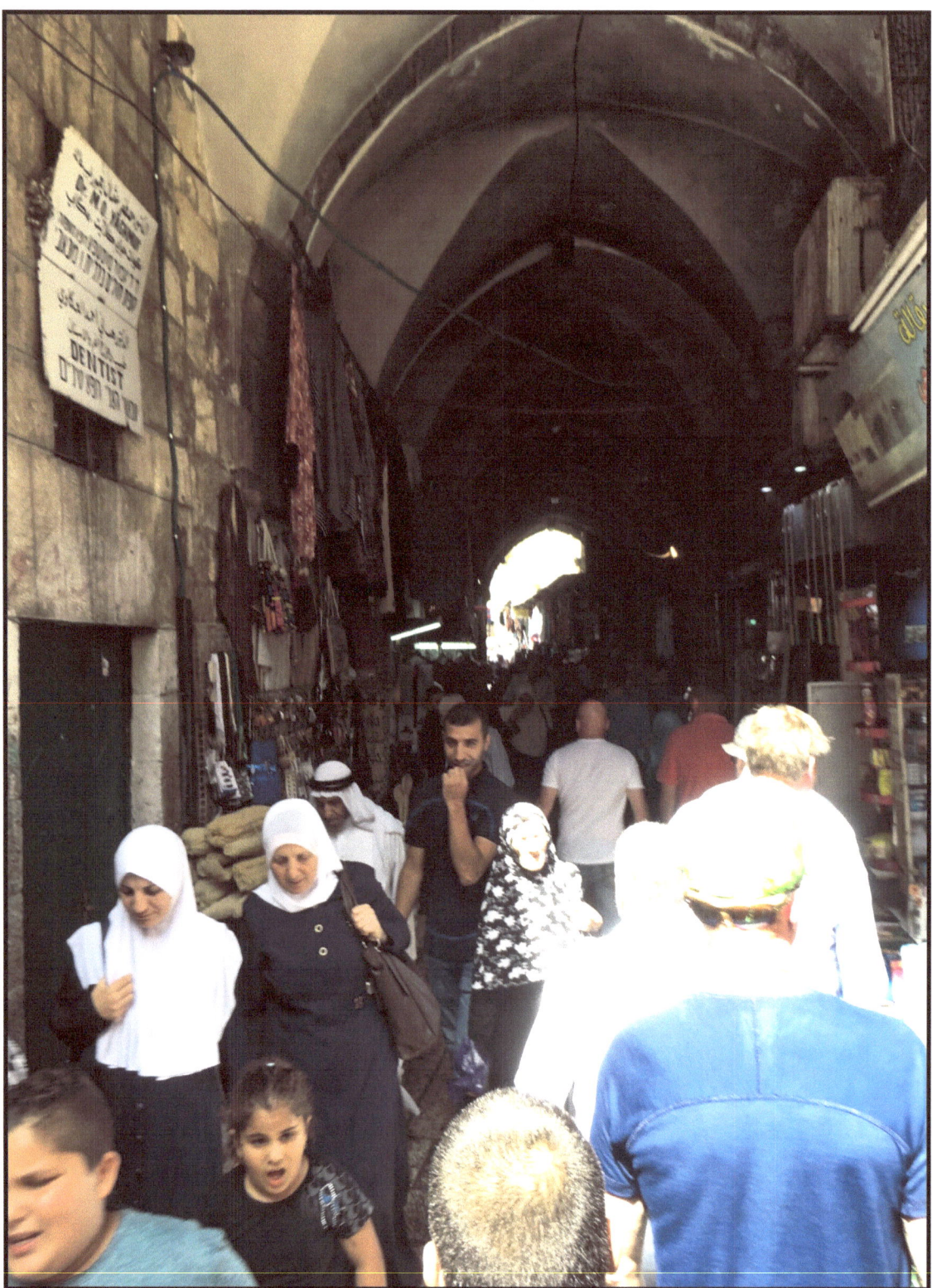

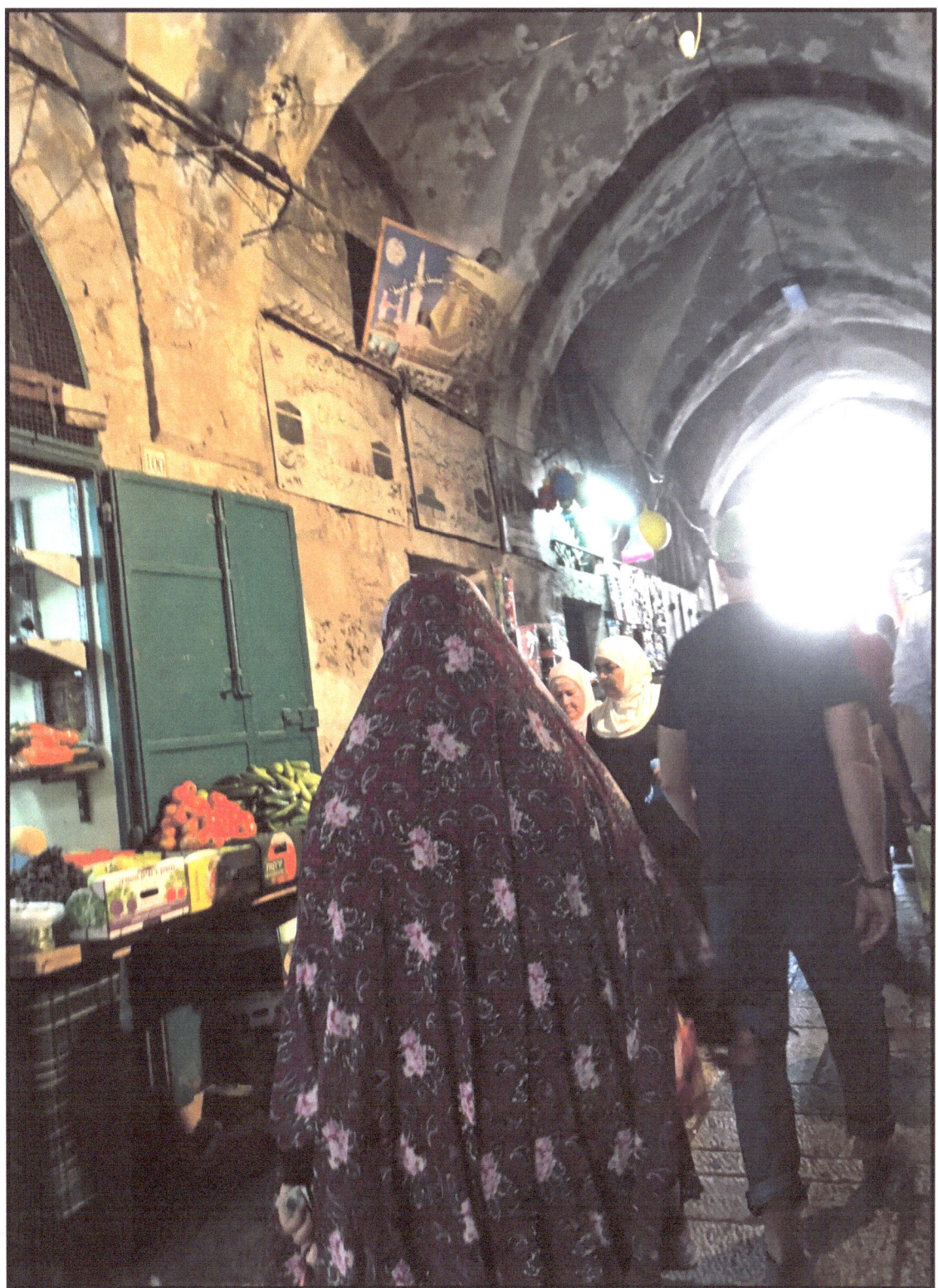

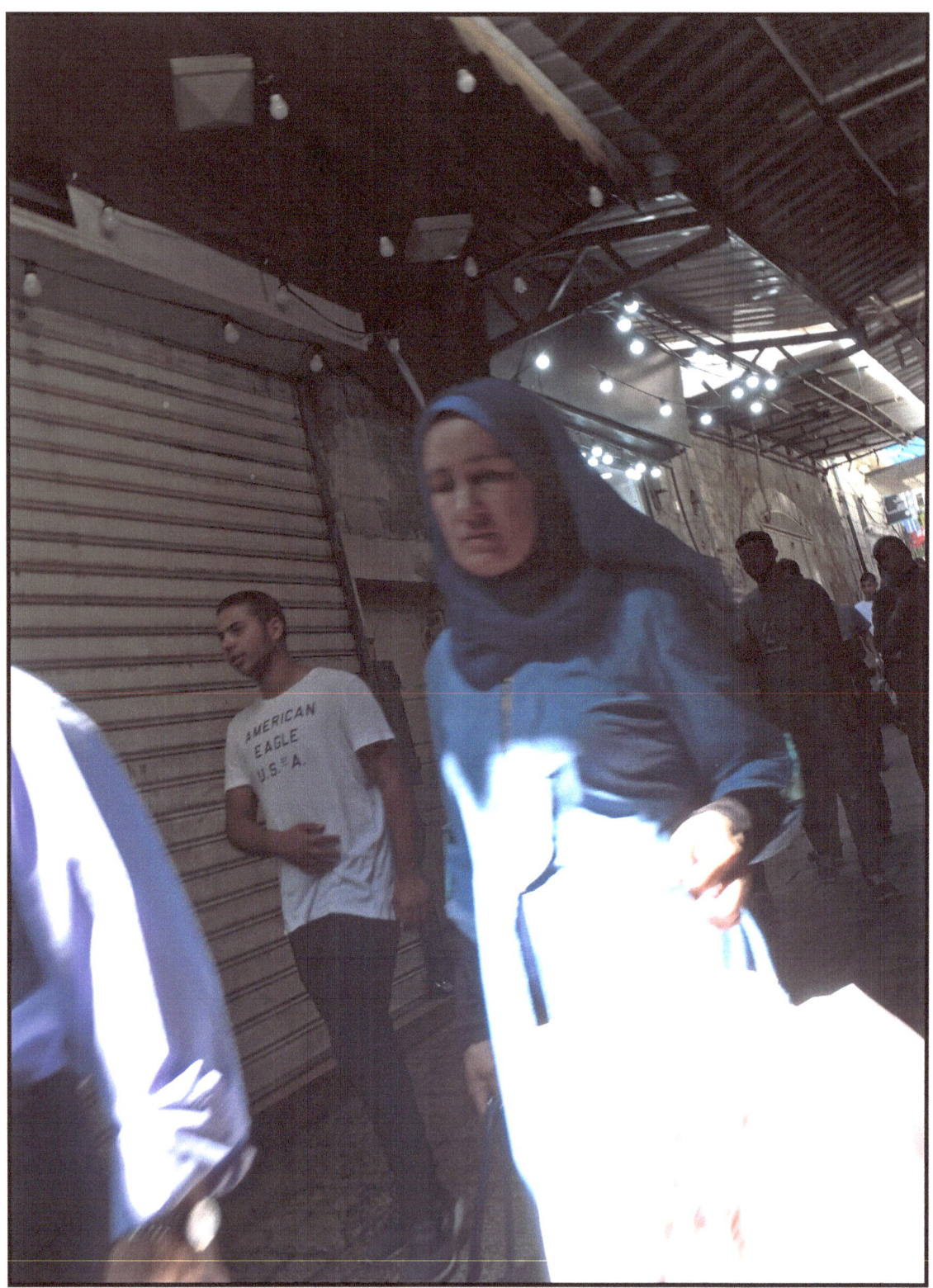

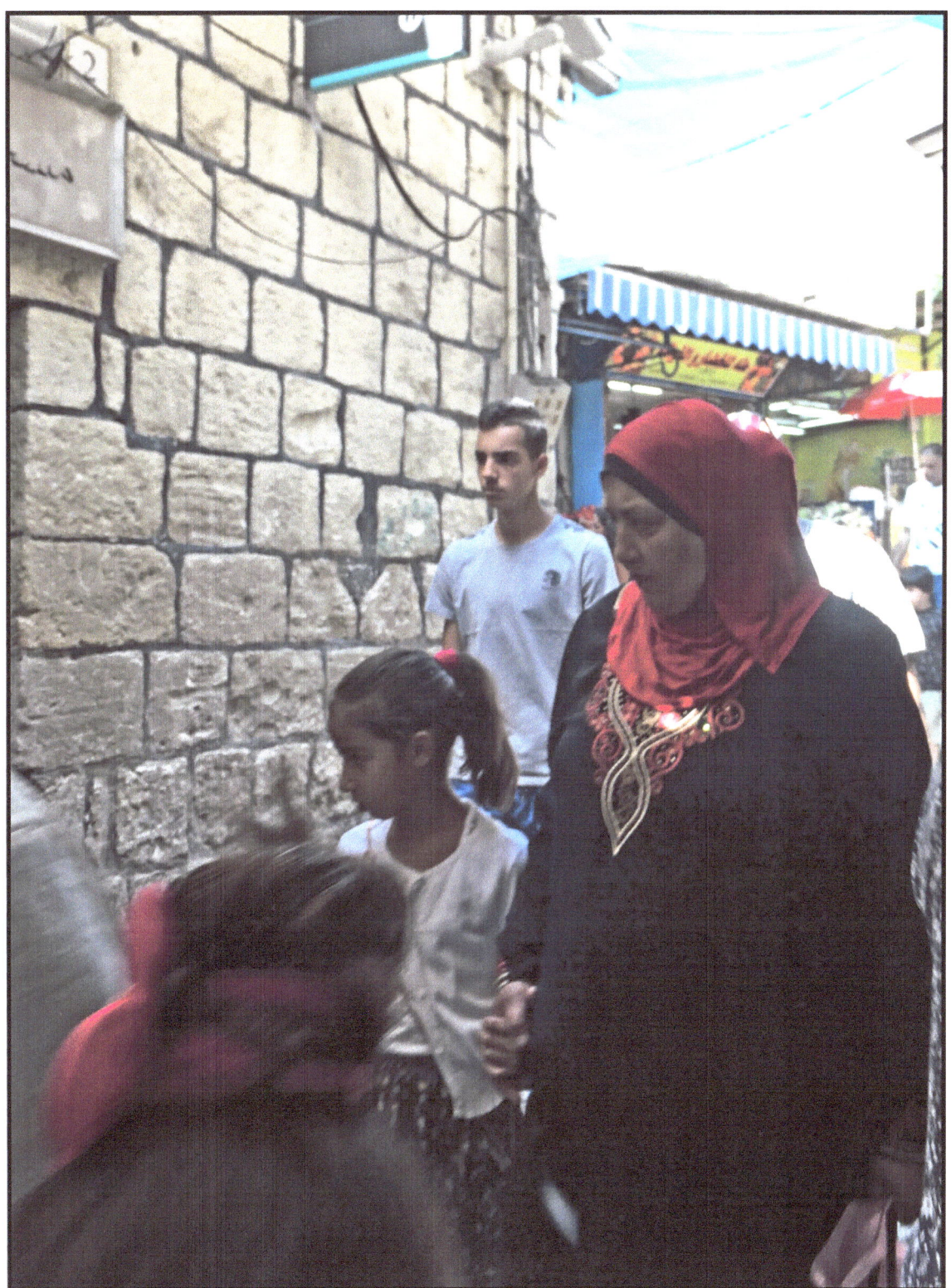

Tel Aviv

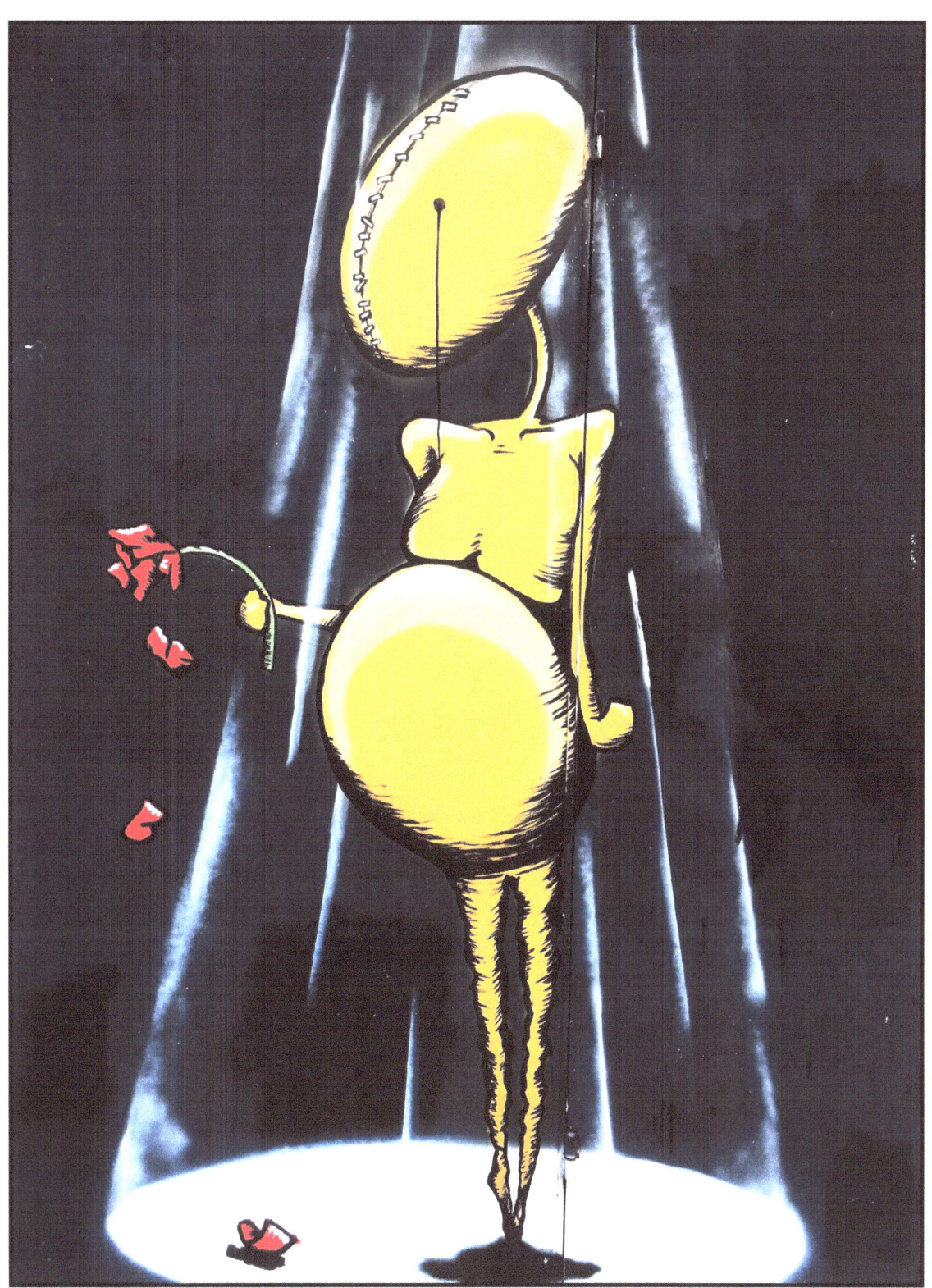

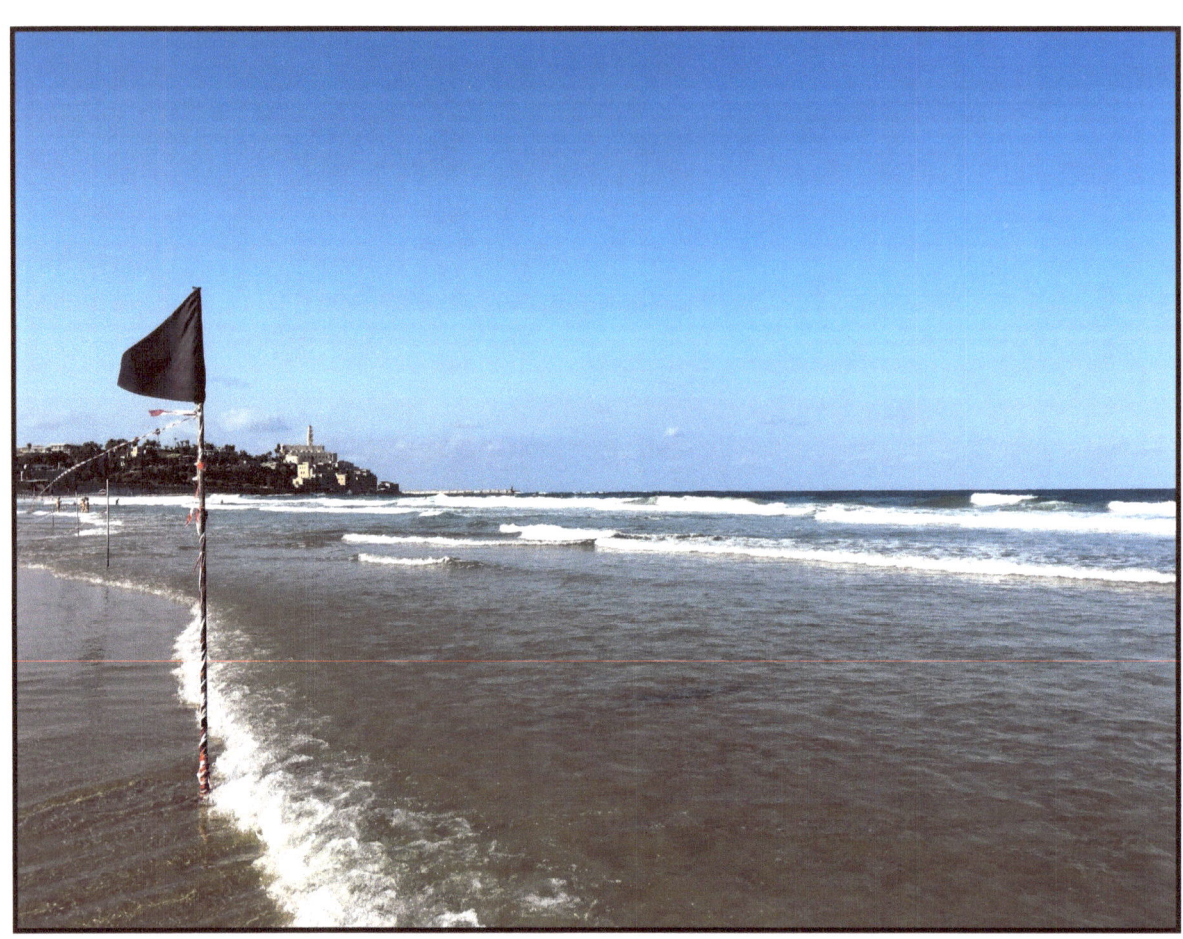

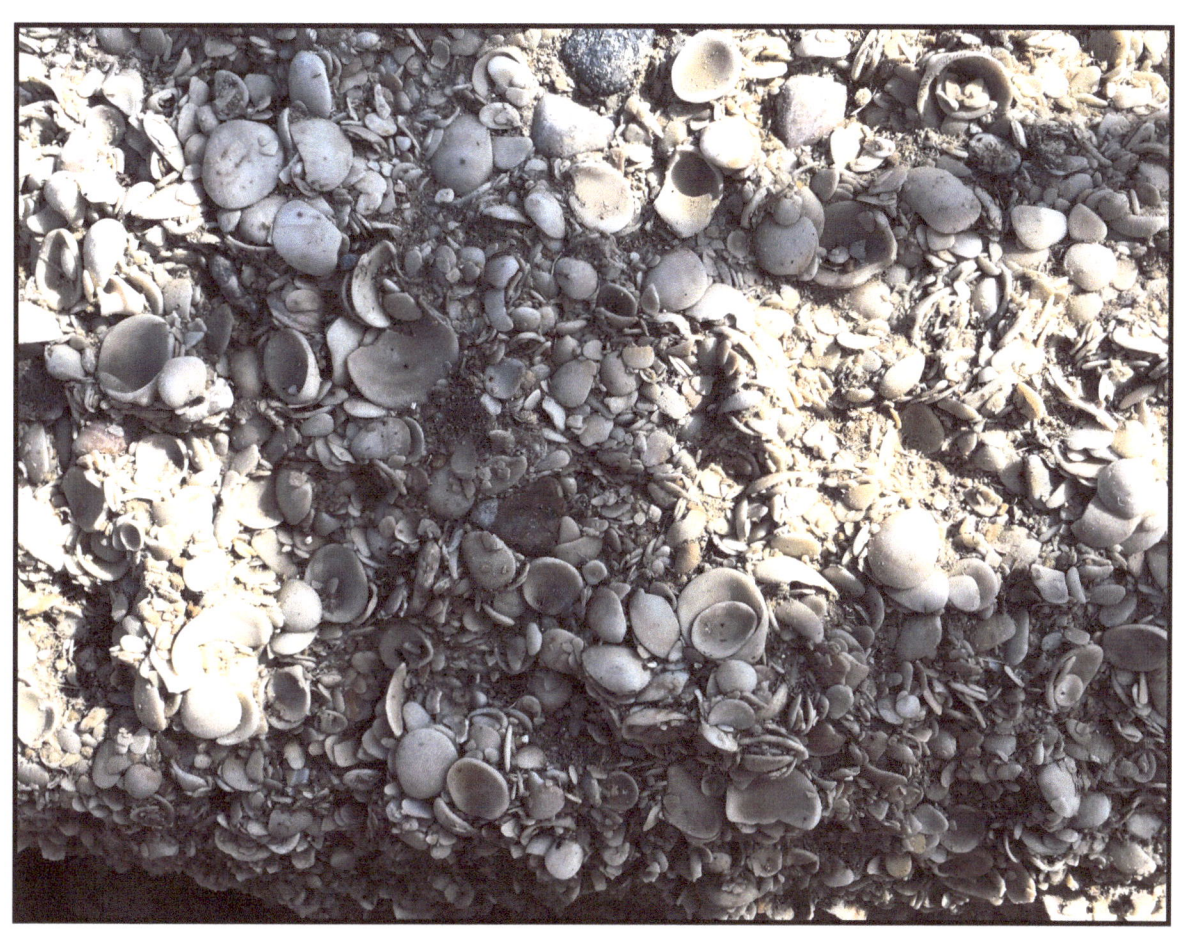

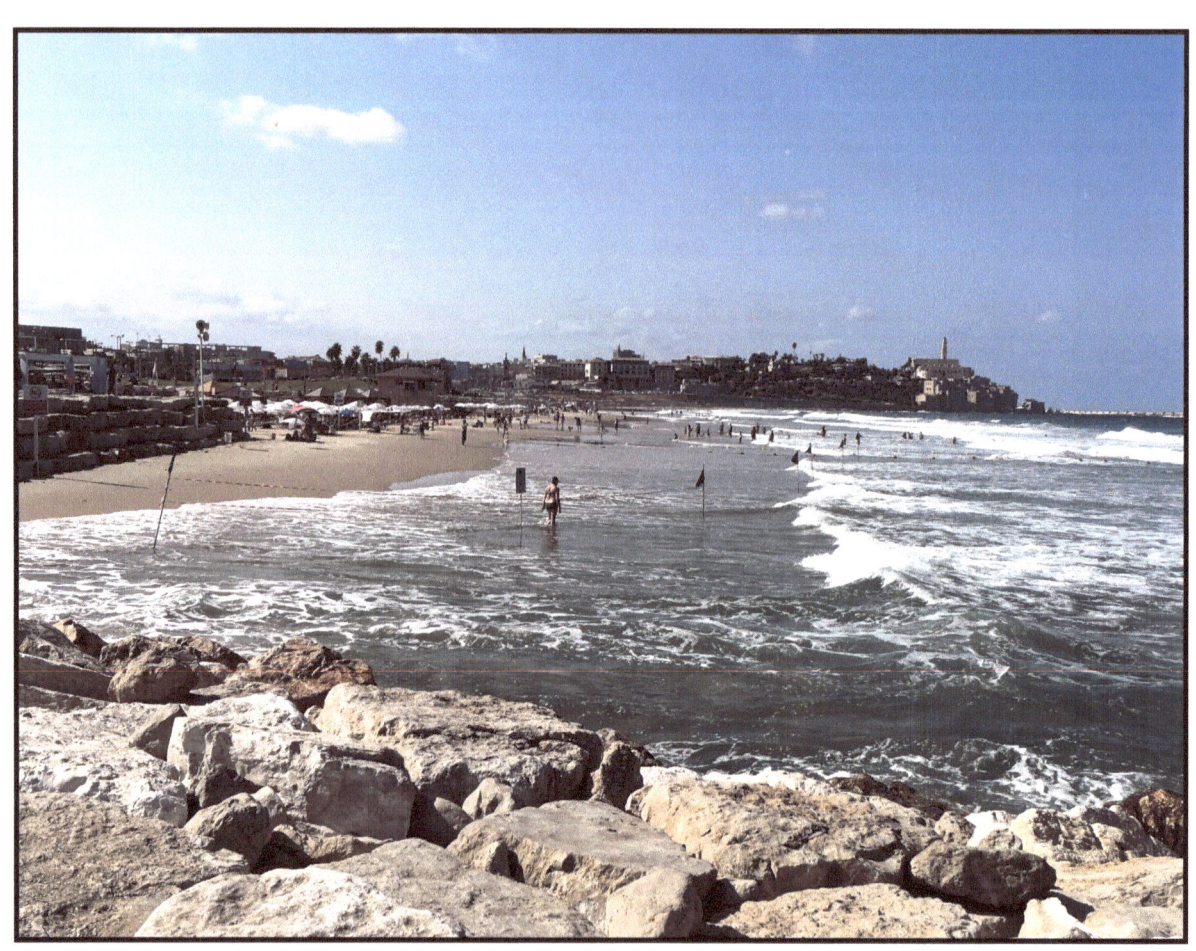

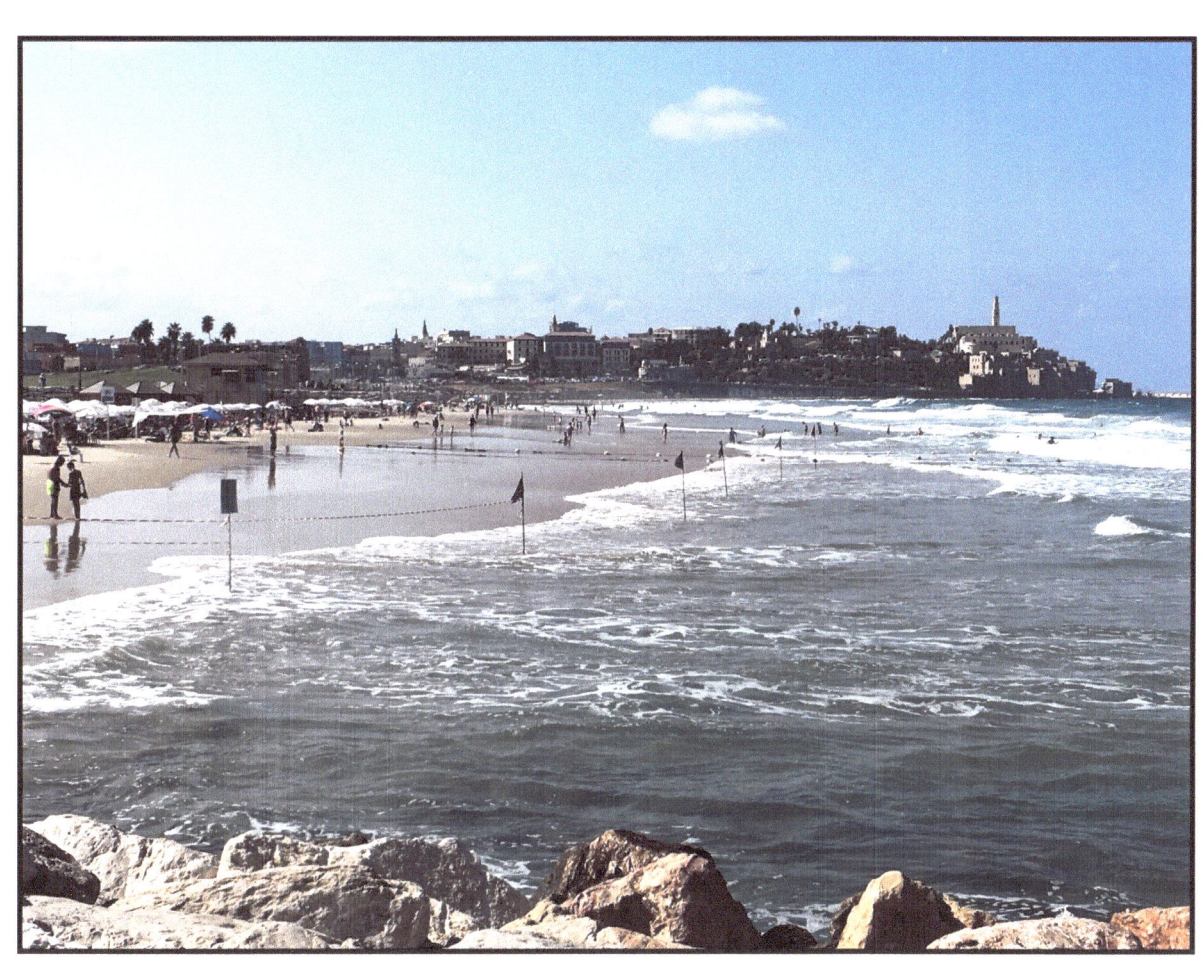

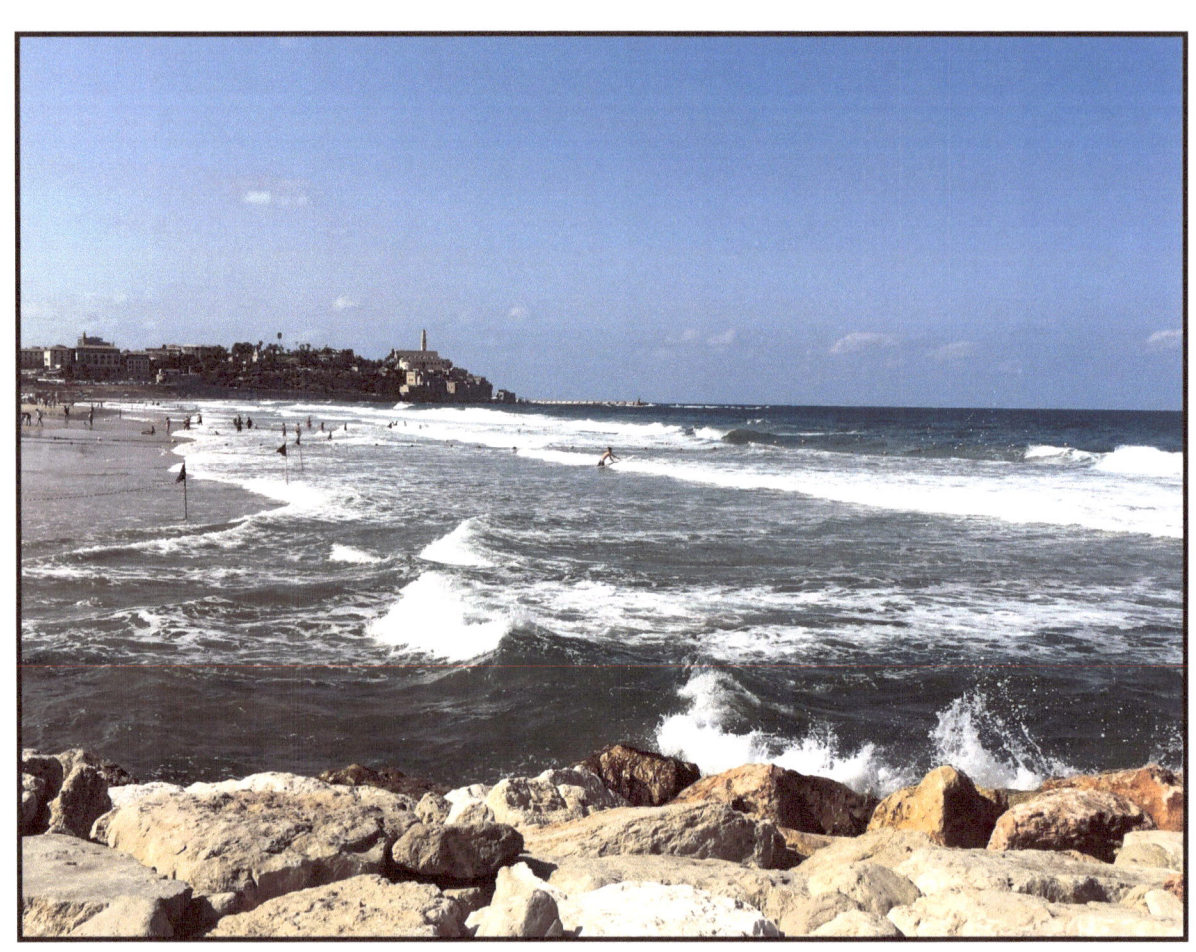

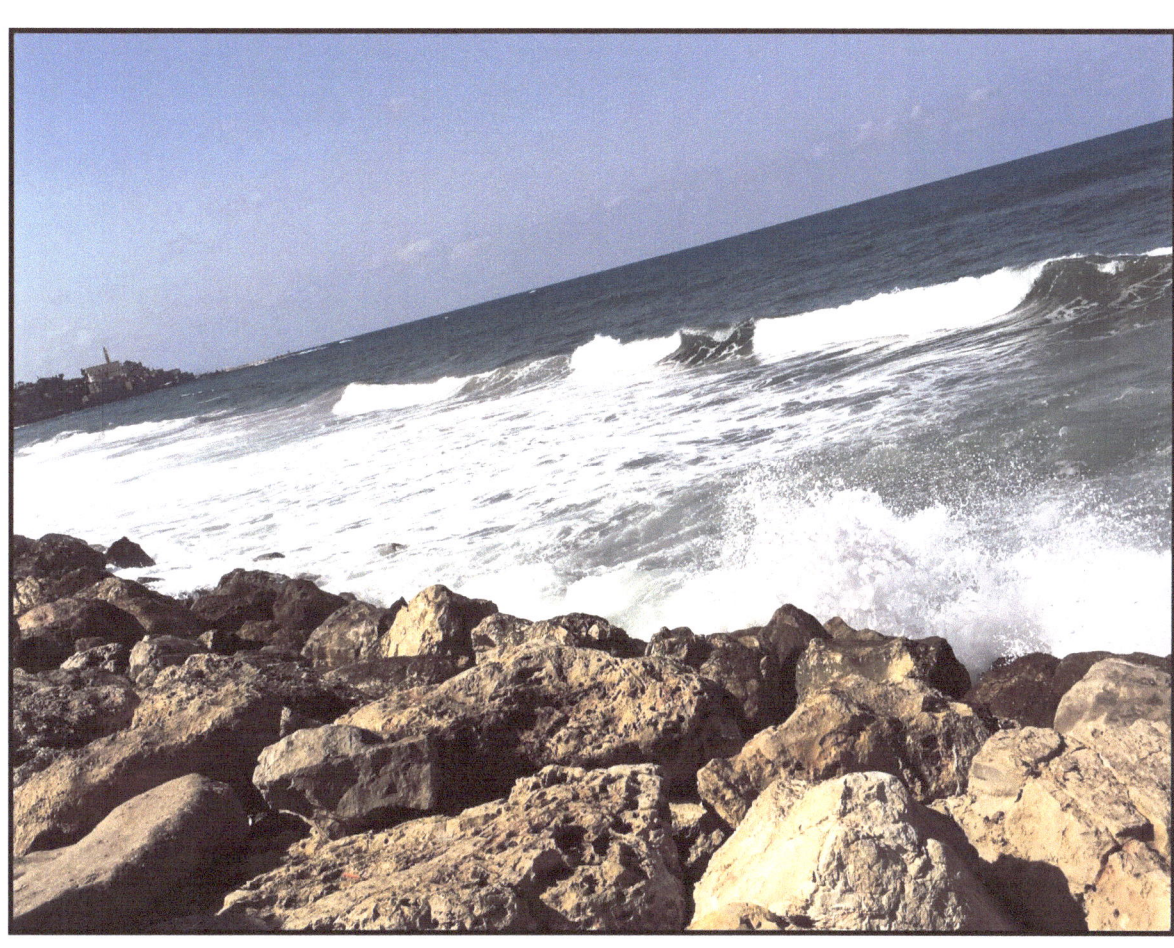

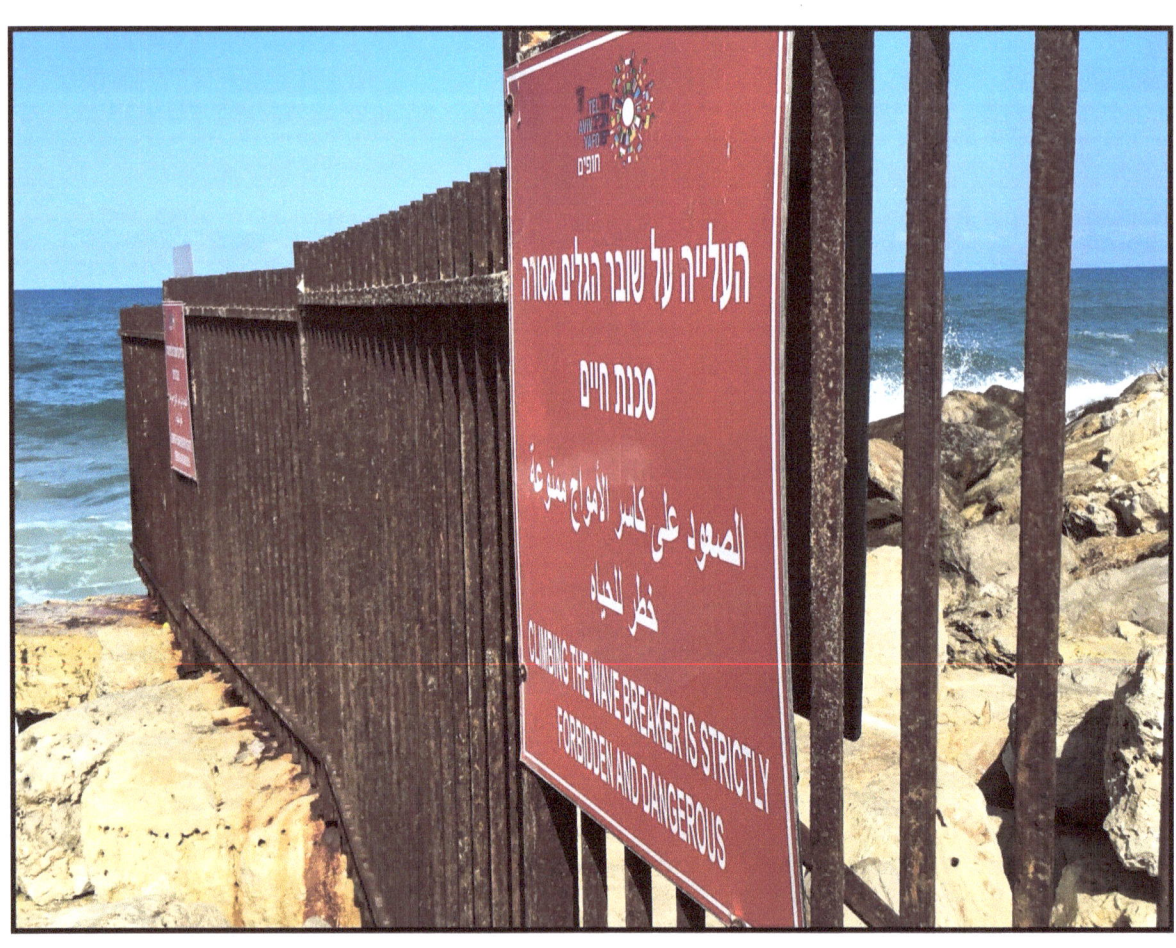

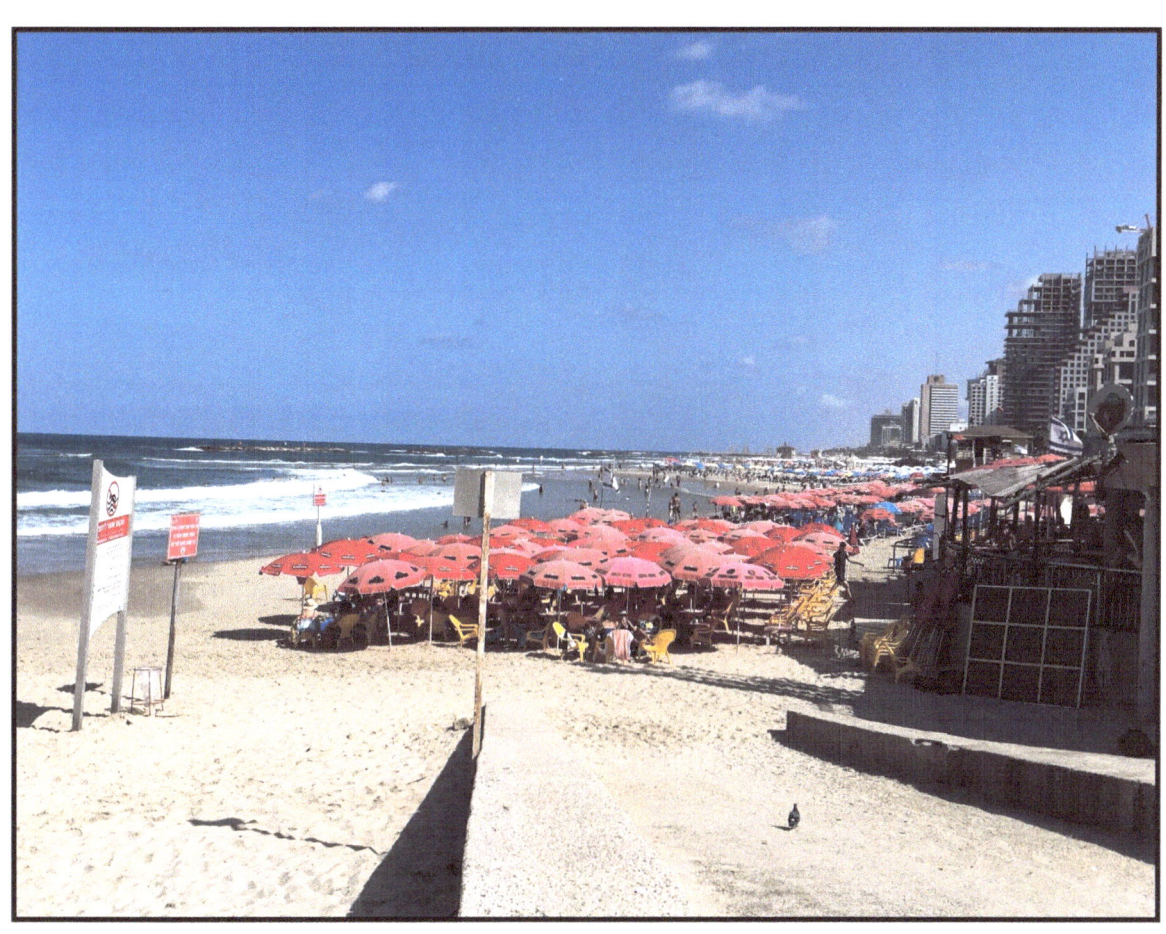

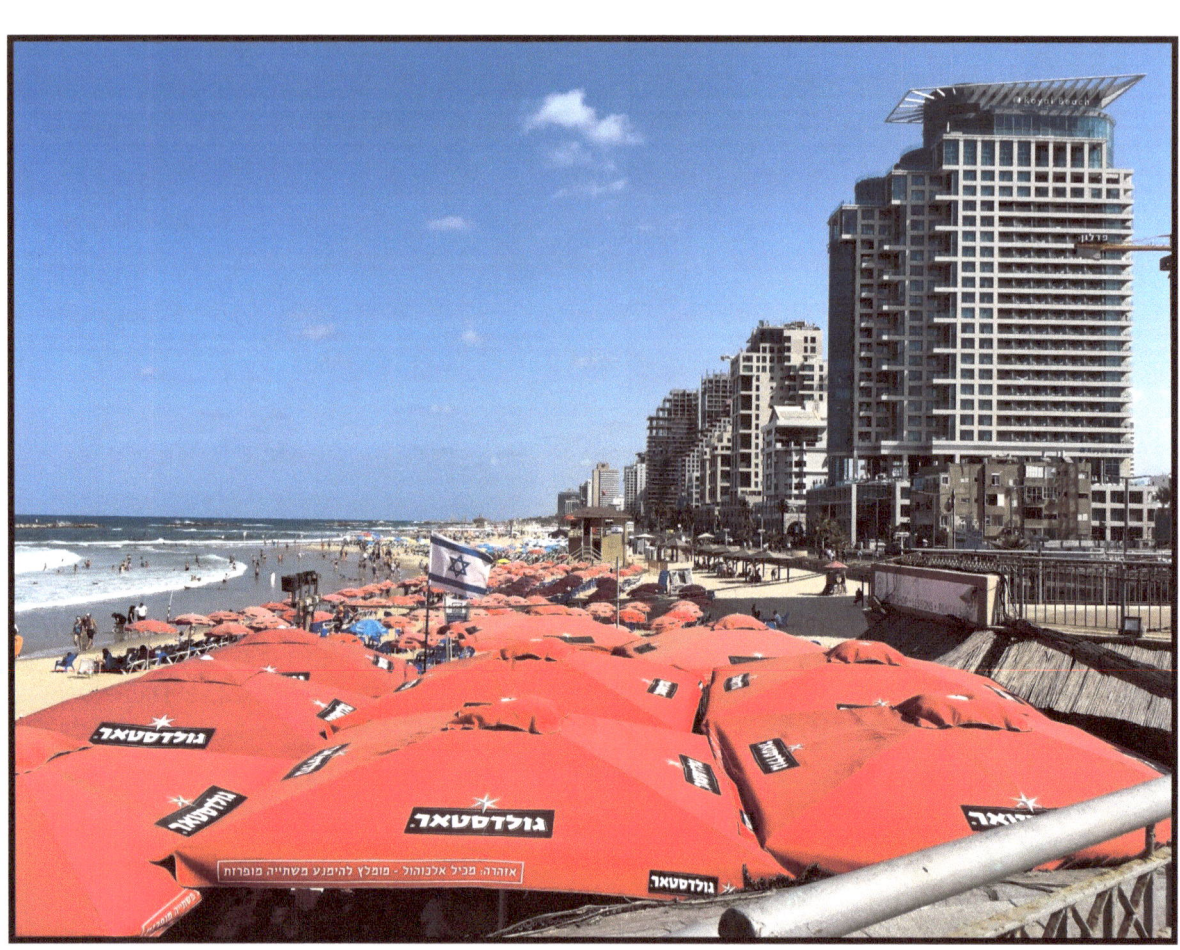

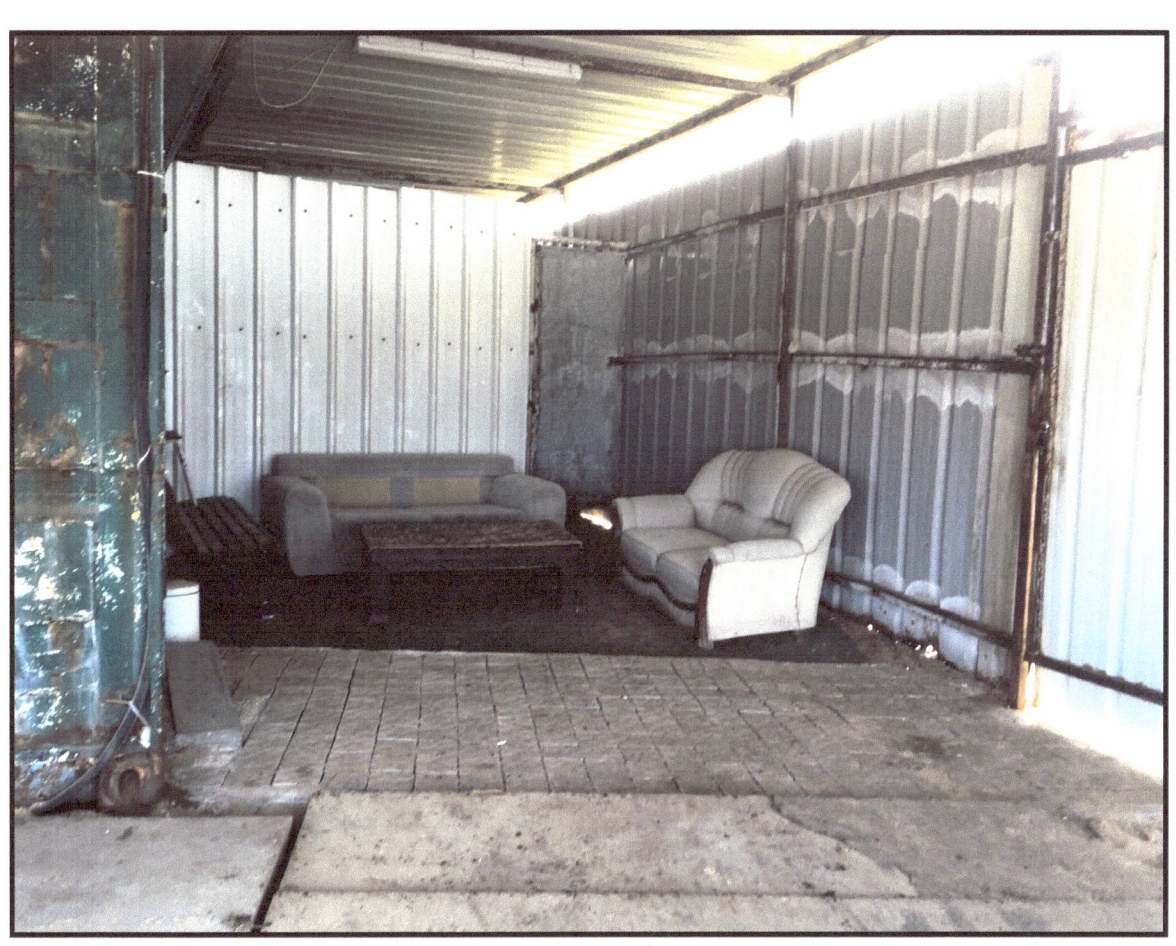

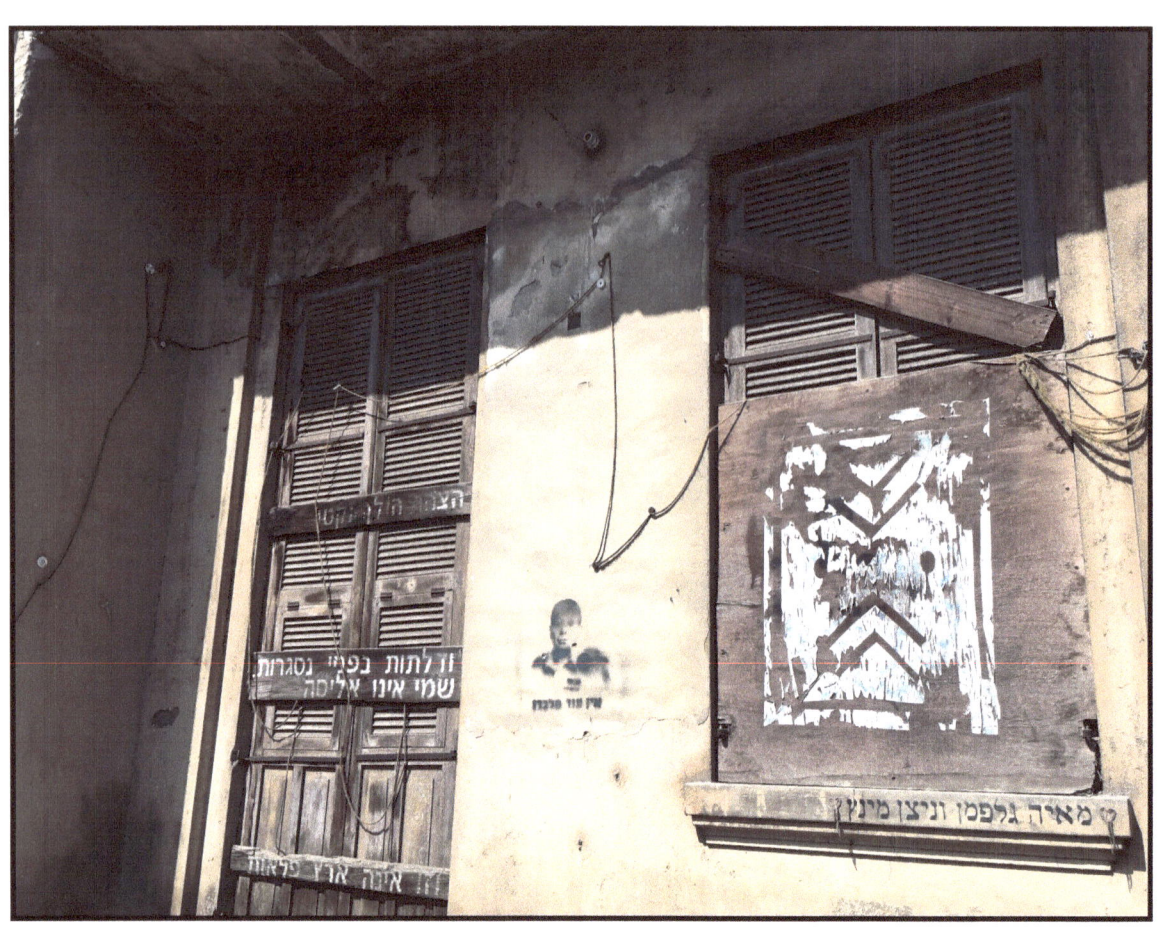

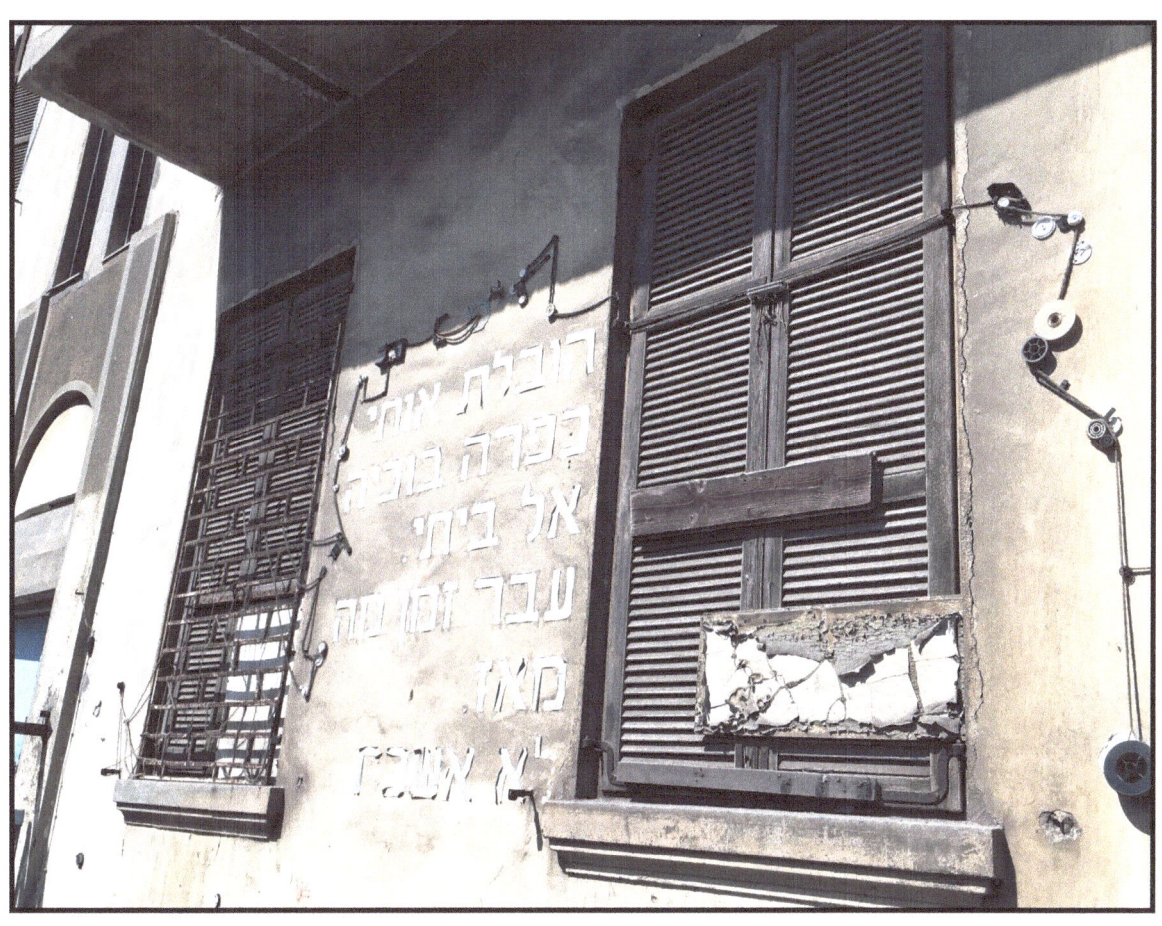

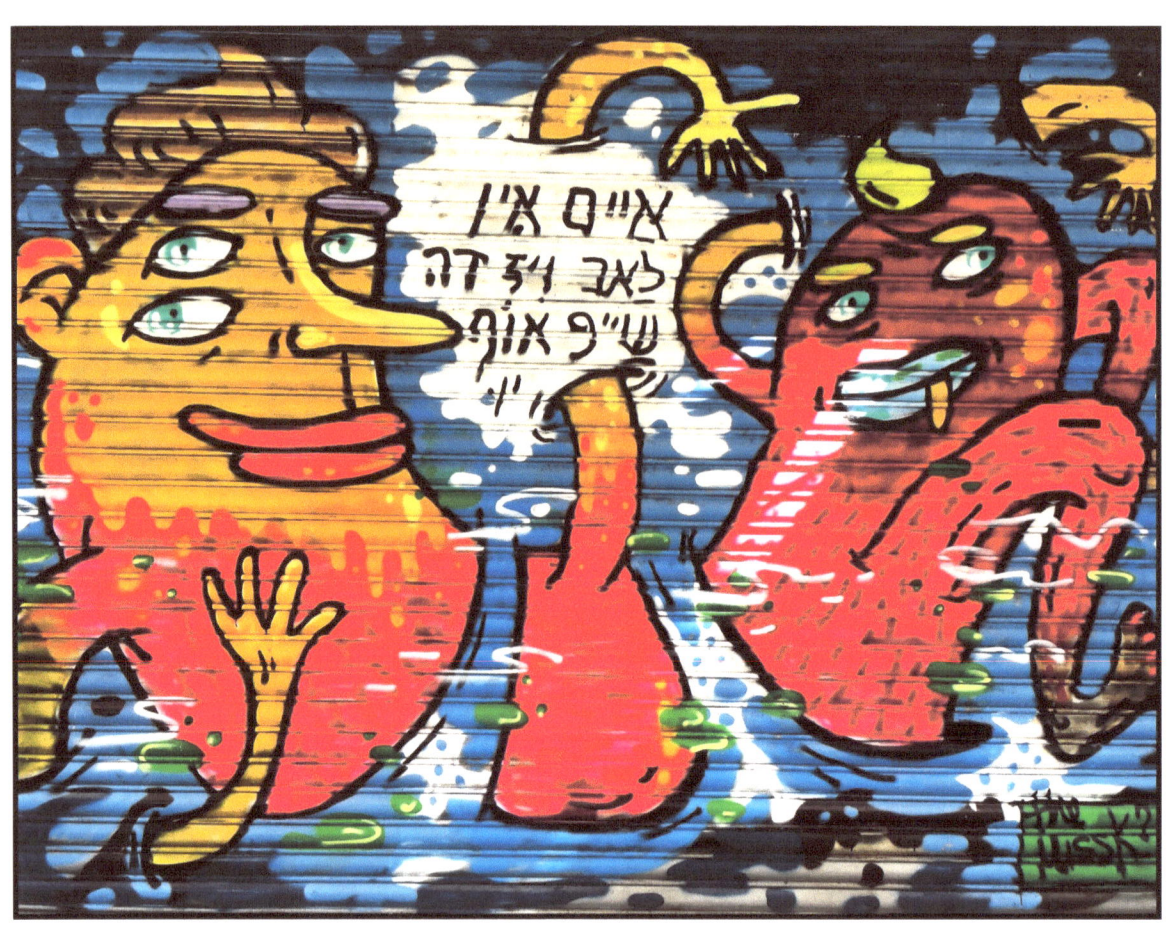

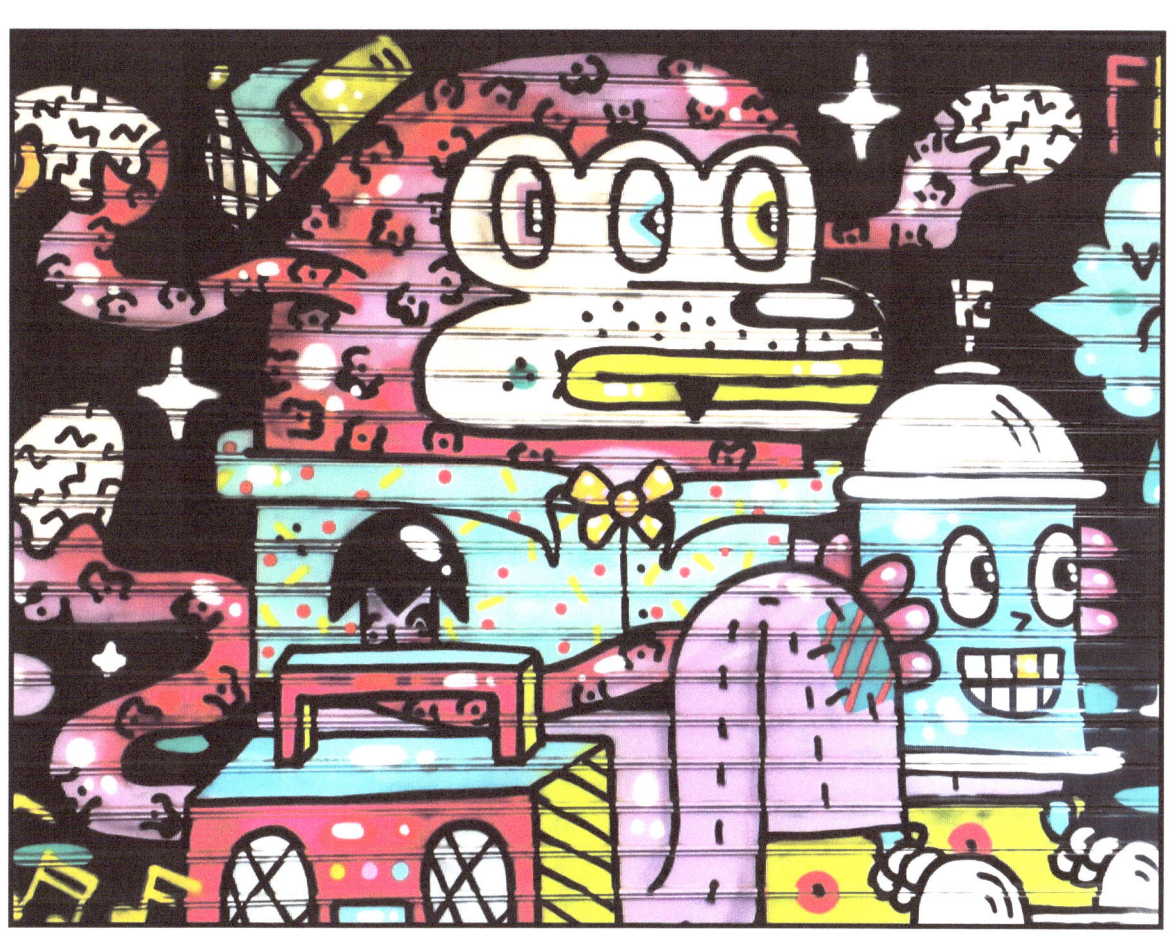

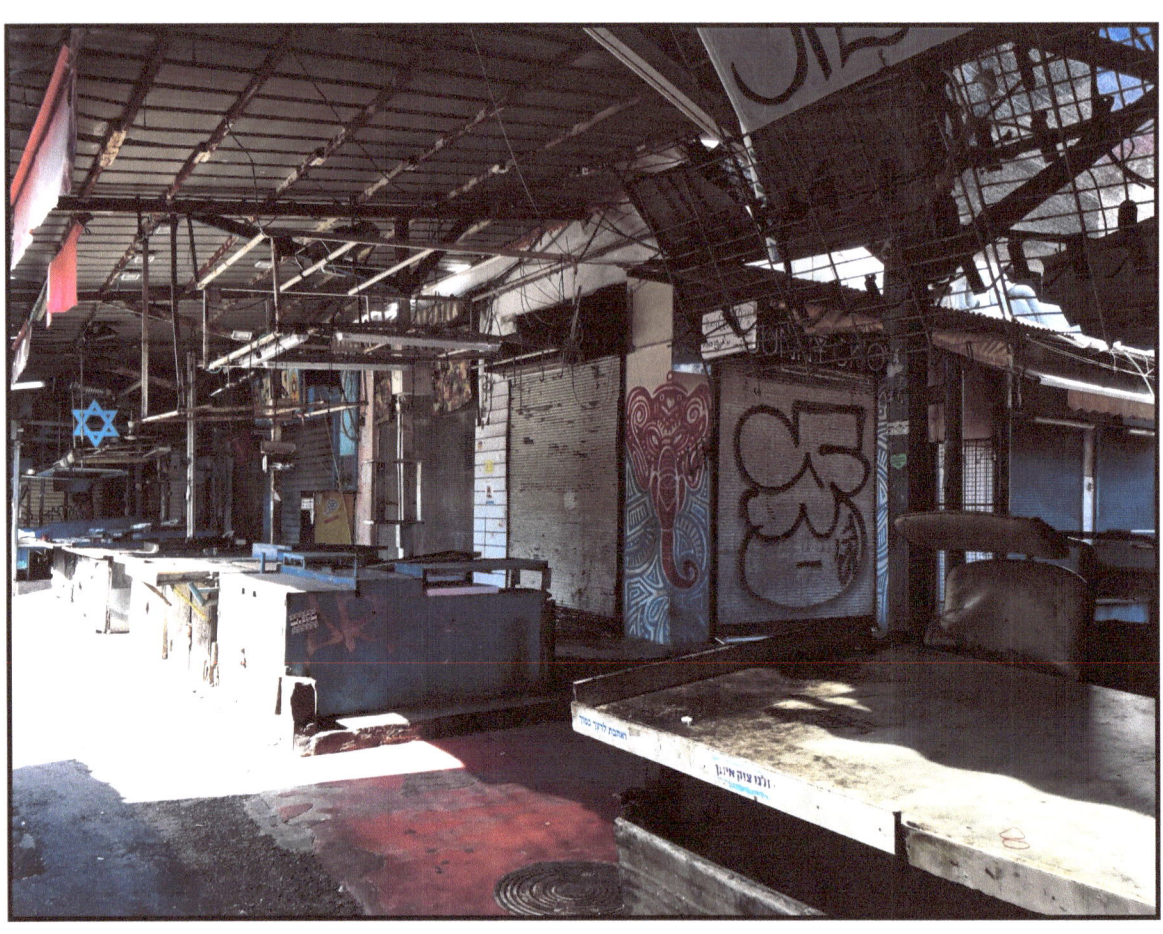

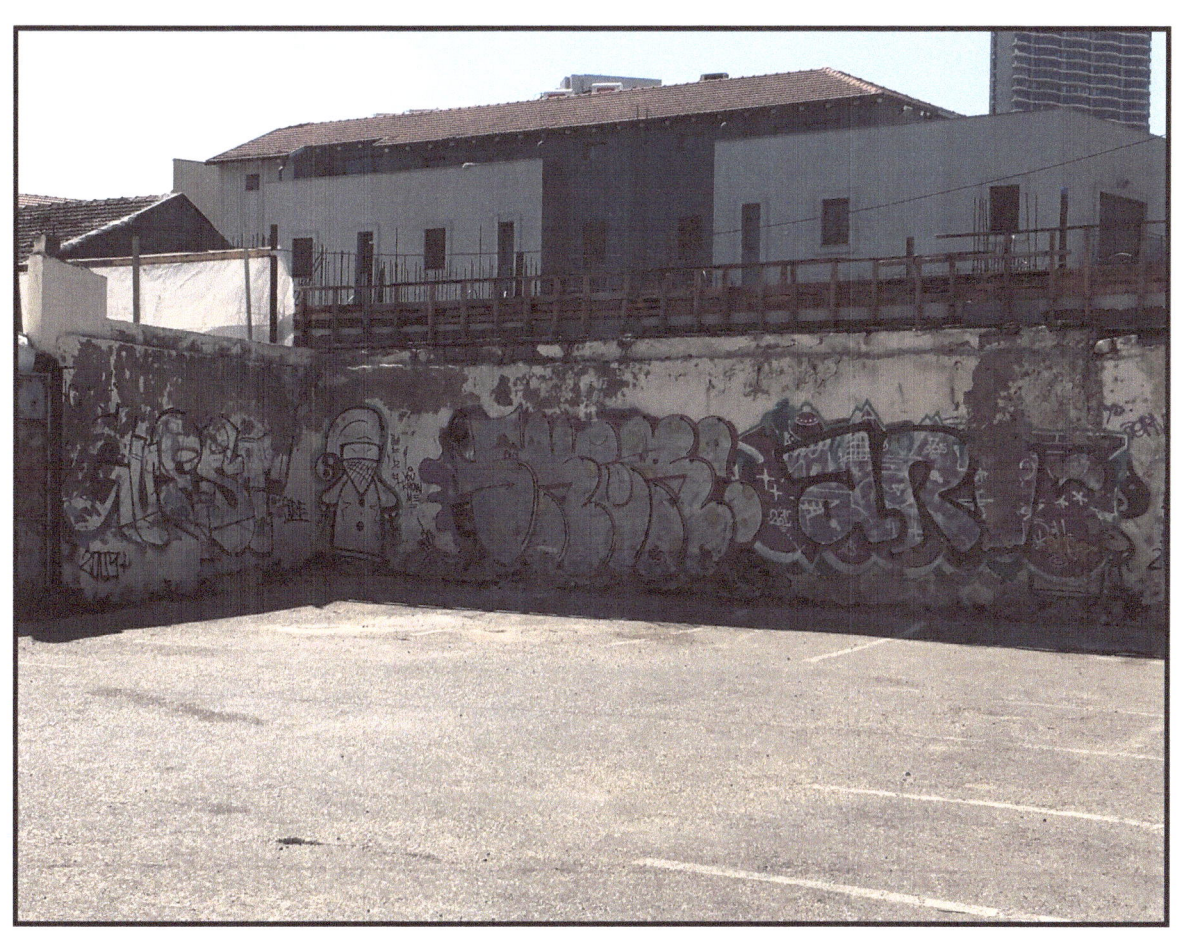

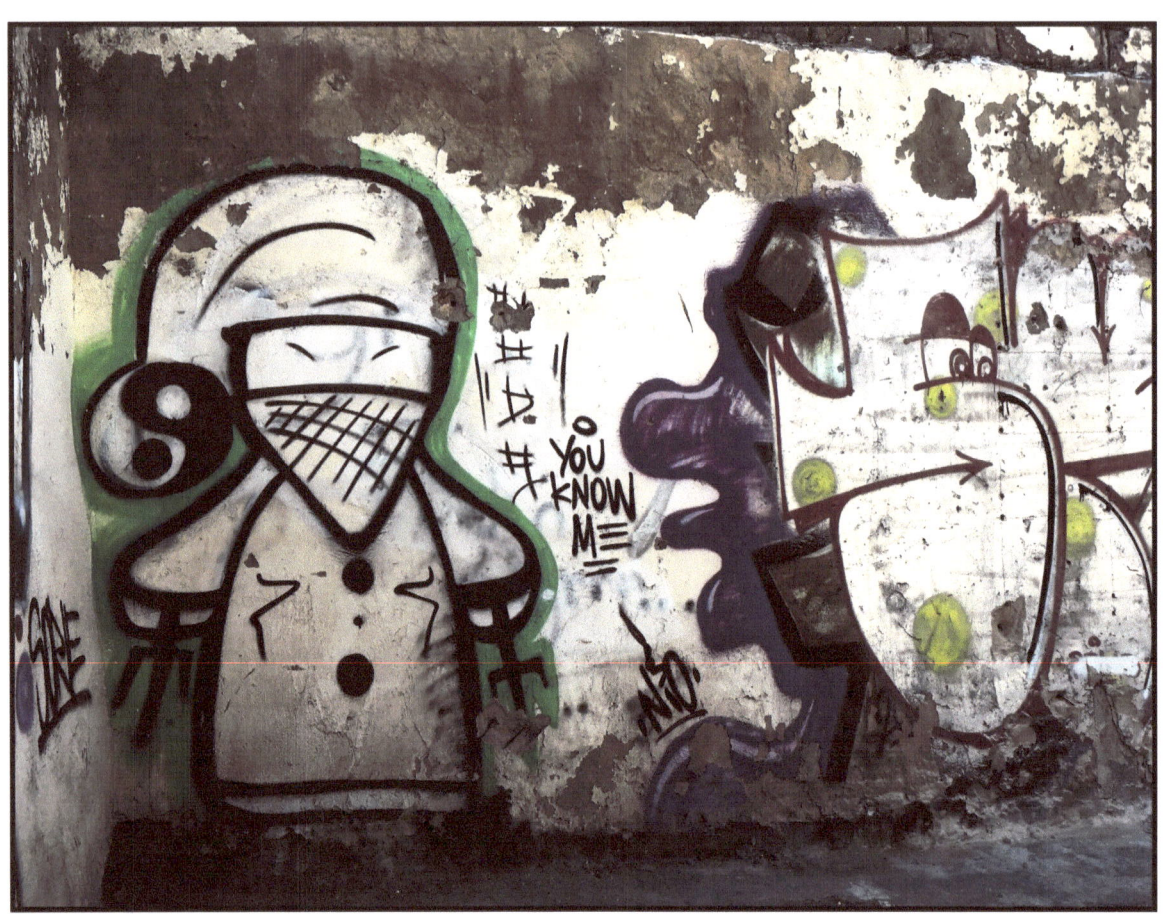

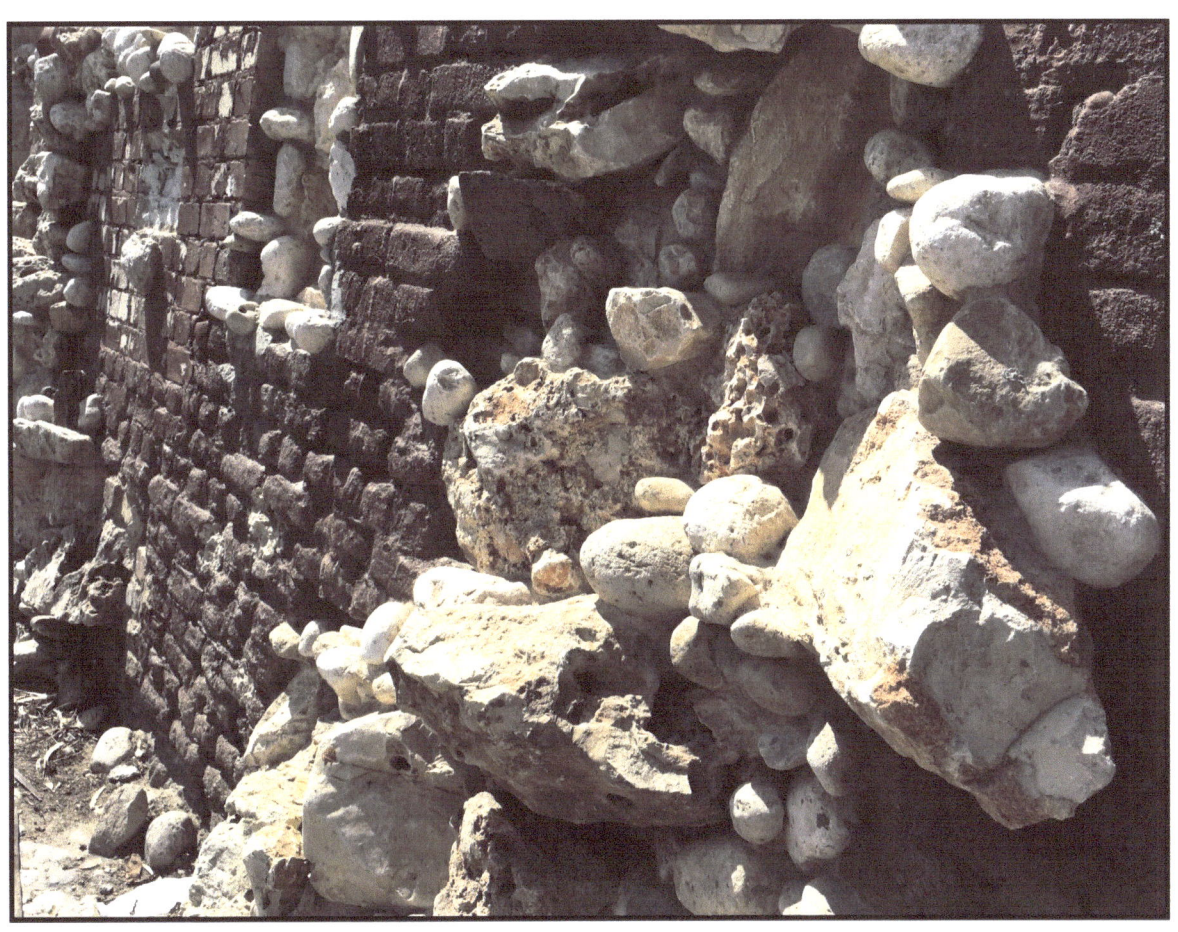

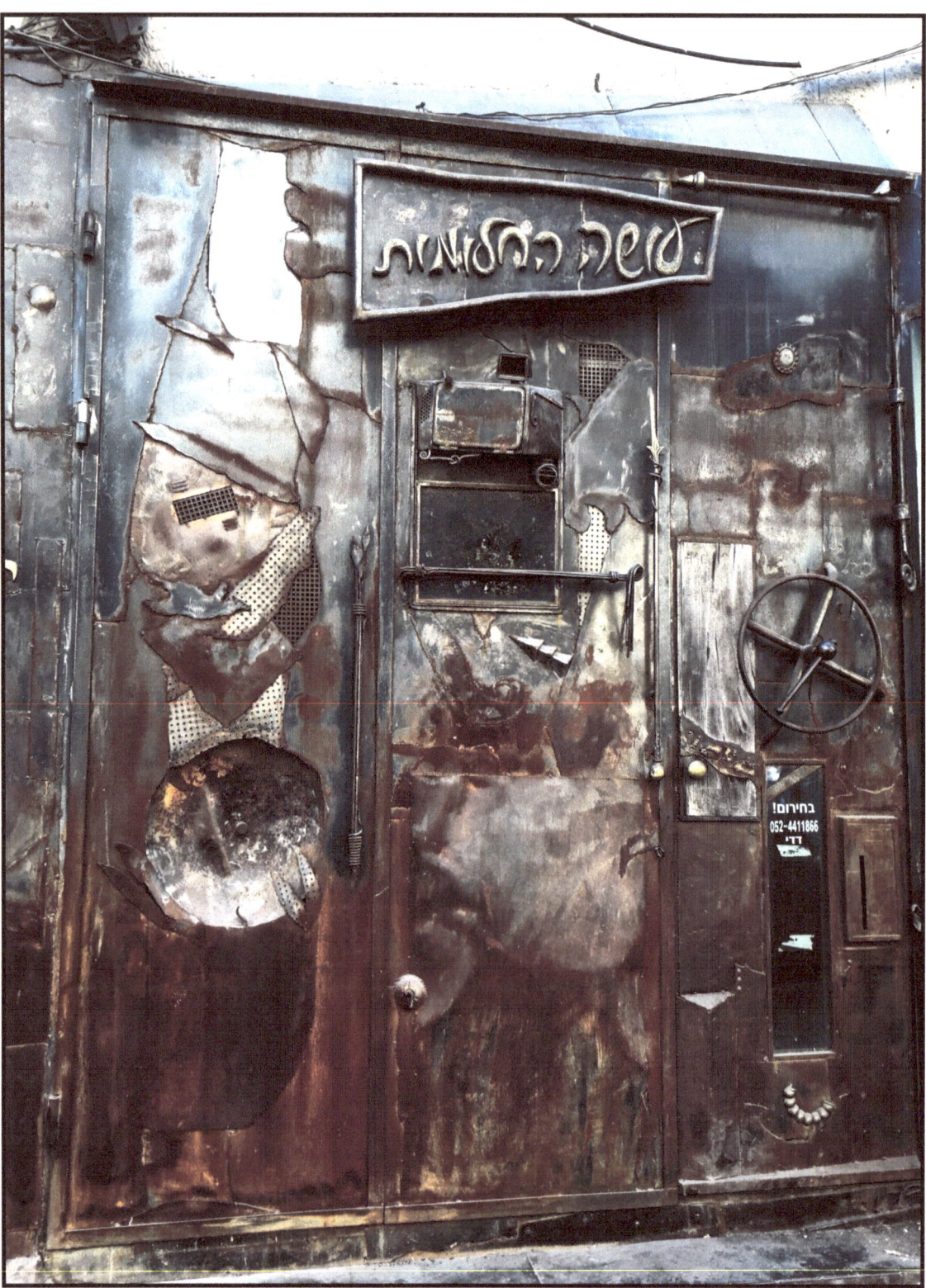

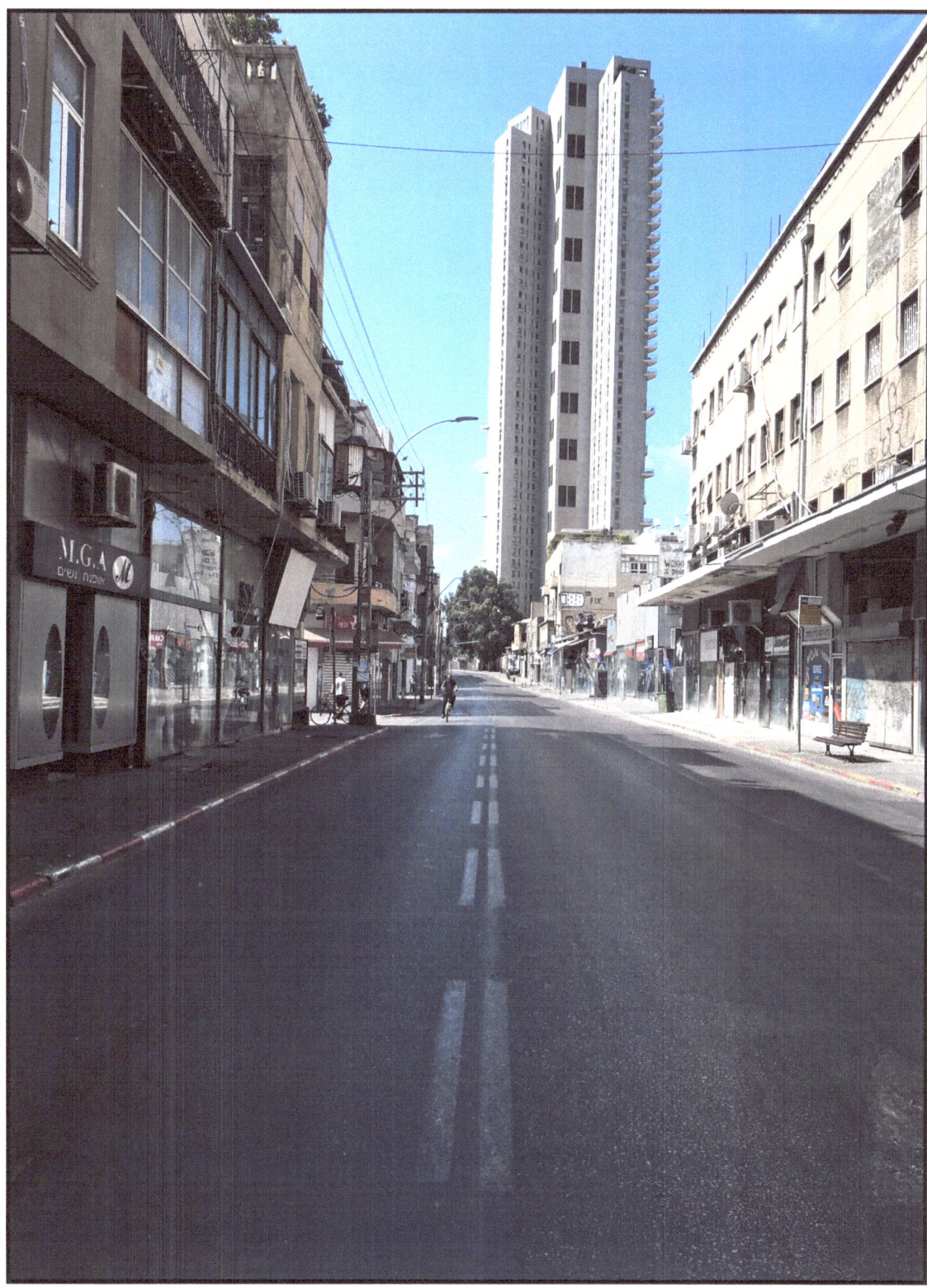

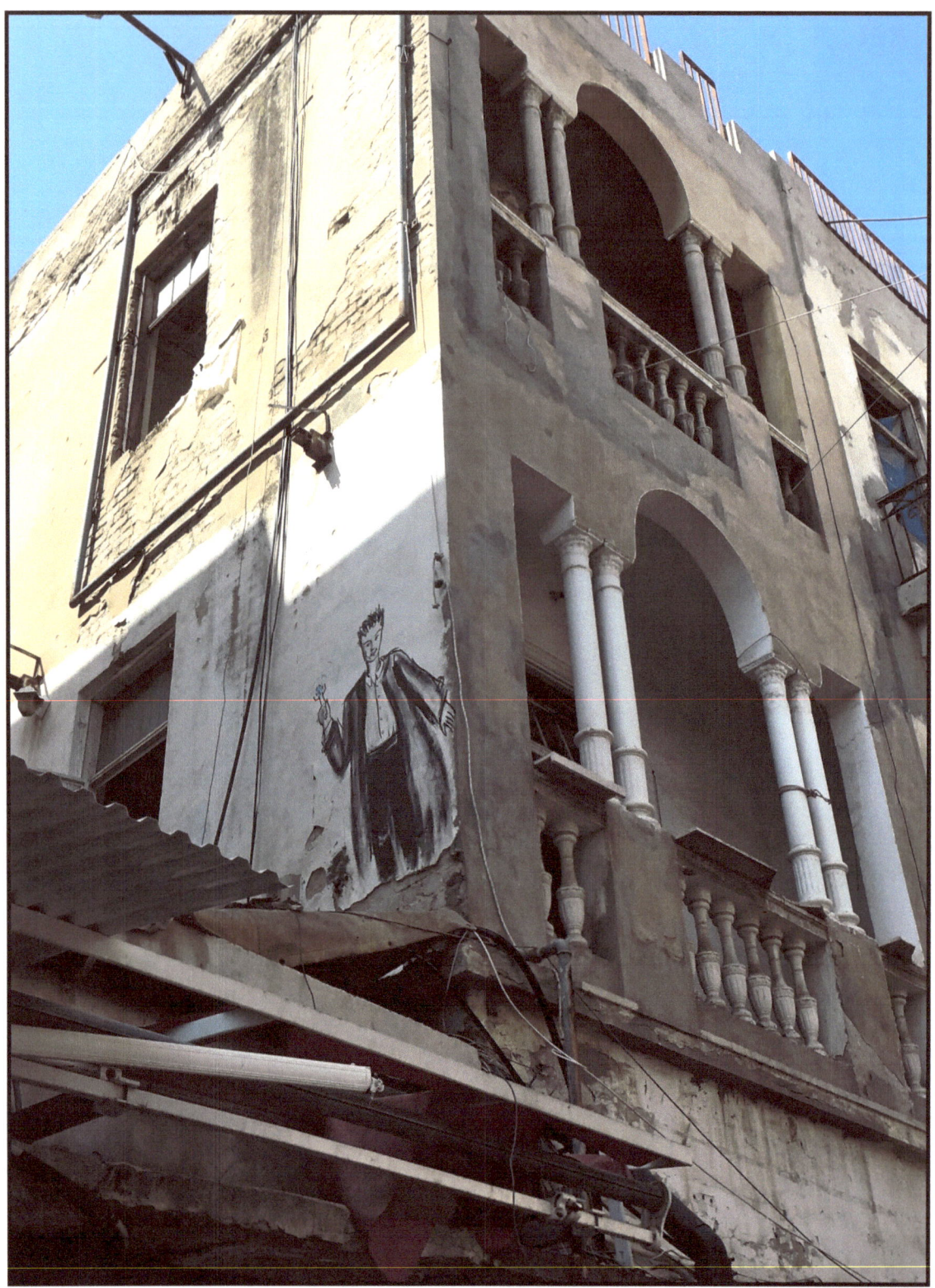

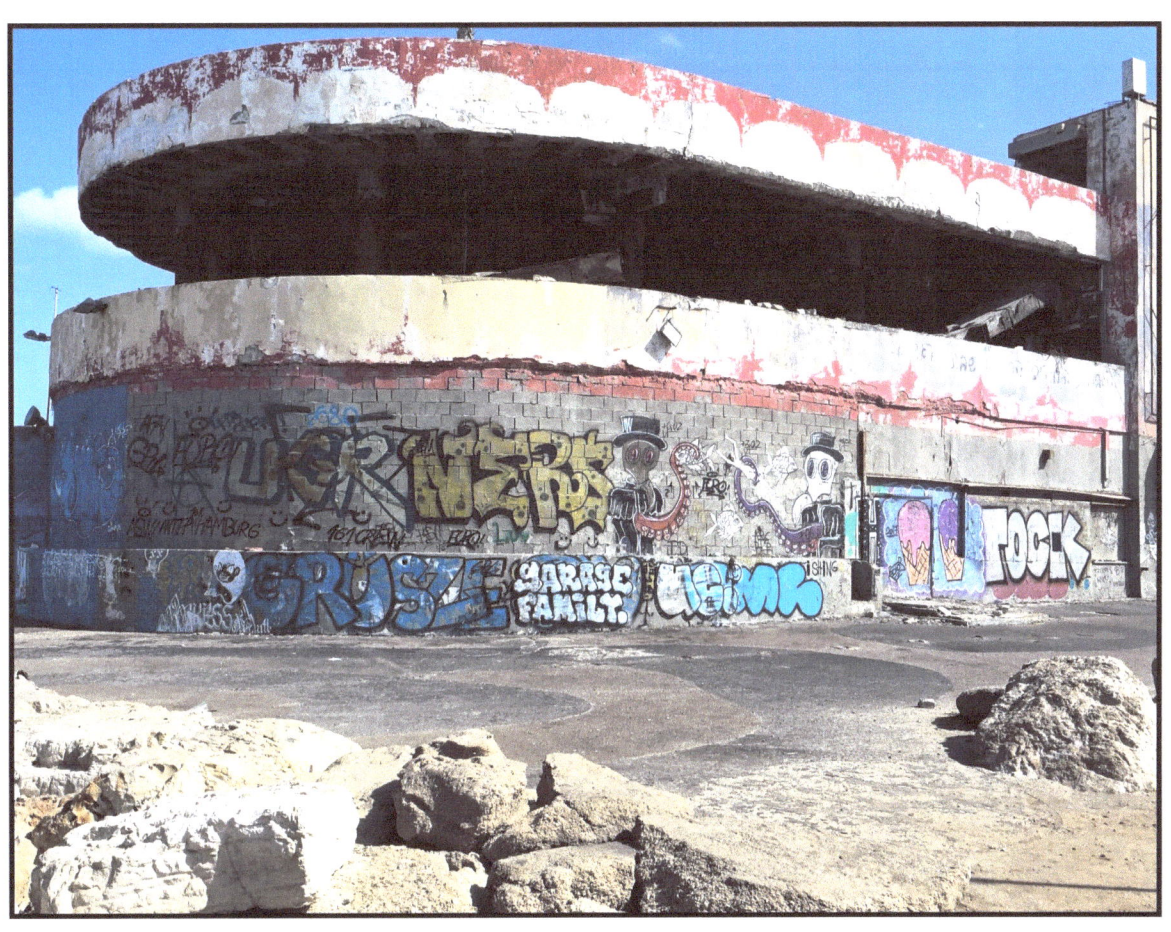

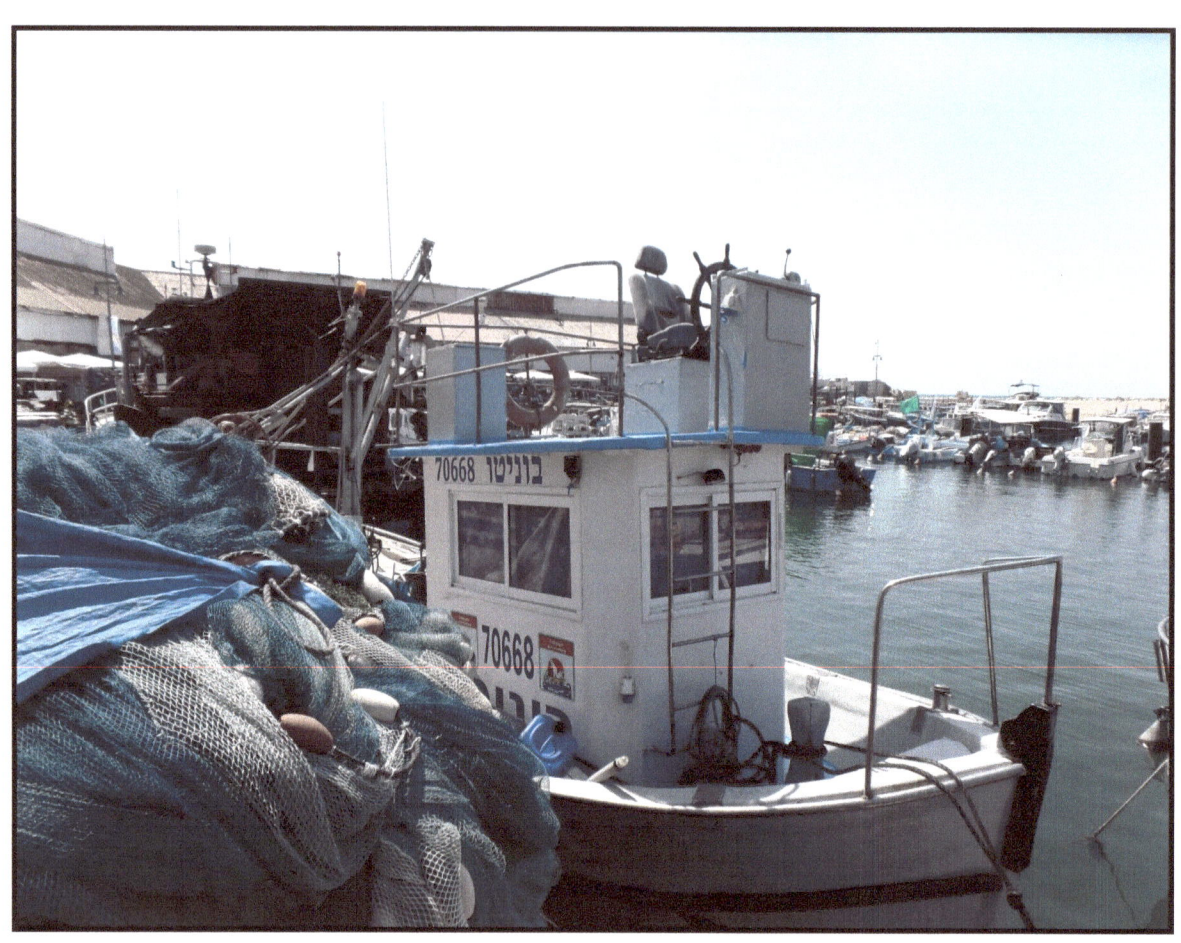

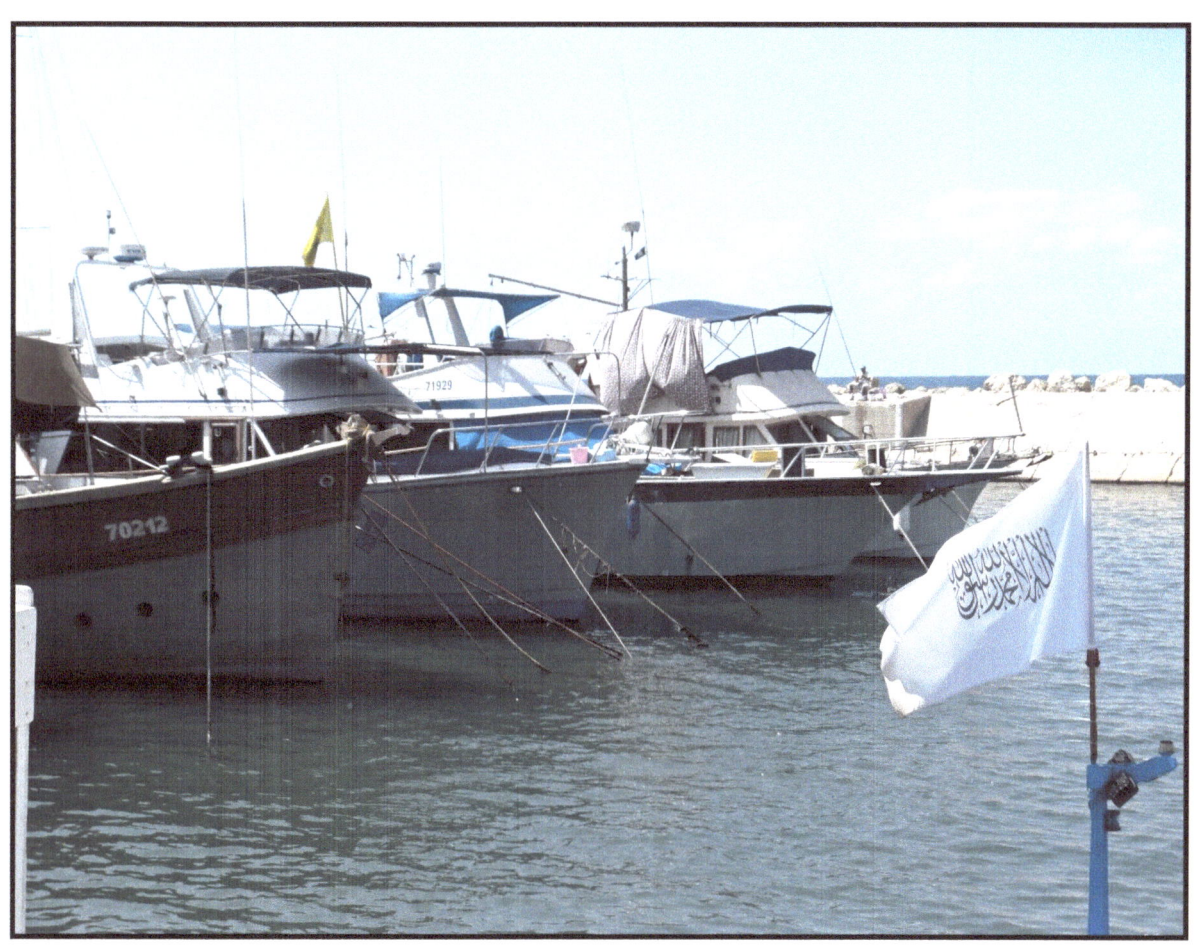

The End

www.ingramcontent.com/pod-product-compliance
Lightning Source LLC
Chambersburg PA
CBHW051153220526
45473CB00003B/761